30μ

D0871201

The Secrets
of the
Shakespeare Sonnets

Printed in Great Britain for The Mitre Press (Fudge & Co. Ltd.),
by The Knole Park Press Ltd., Sevenoaks, Kent.

BACON AT THE AGE OF EIGHTEEN YEARS.

(From the portrait by Hilliard.)

The Secrets of the Shakespeare Sonnets

BY

RODERICK L. EAGLE

With facsimile reproduction of the 1609 edition of the Sonnets and " A Lover's Complaint ".

"We have set it down as a law to ourselves to examine things to the bottom; and not to receive upon credit, or reject upon improbabilities, until there have been passed a due examination."

Francis Bacon.

LONDON :

THE MITRE PRESS

52 LINCOLN'S INN FIELDS, W.C.2

To Evelyn

"You are my true and honourable wife."

(*Julius Caesar* II, i.)

Contents

Introduction

WE are all attracted by the fascination of the mysterious. Newspaper editors, experienced in gauging what is likely to impress and excite their millions of readers, deal with the commonplace briefly; but if the circumstances are unusual and baffling, the matter will be given prominent headlines. The different kinds and degrees of crime provide clear examples of what I mean. There is something of the detective in most of us, and there have been cases where the amateur has been able to provide the professionals with an important clue when expert investigation has failed.

Since the first publication of the Shakespeare Sonnets in 1609, innumerable literary students have attempted to solve the enigmas contained in the 2,000 lines of verse, and not one of the recognised experts, who has entered this maze, has been able to find the centre. They have built up a library of conjecture, and a perplexing array of contradictory theories, not one of which will bear close examination by anybody who has made a special study of the literature, history and the state of society of those times. In 1817, Nathan Drake invented the theory that Henry Wriothesley, Earl of Southampton, was the " friend " addressed in the main group of Sonnets, while, in 1832, James Boaden wrote a series of articles in *The Gentleman's Magazine* arguing on behalf of William Herbert, Earl of Pembroke. Lord Southampton was proposed because the poems *Venus and Adonis* and *The Rape of Lucrece* had been dedicated to him in affectionate and intimate terms in 1593 and 1594. The Pembroke theory would never have been put forward but for the fact that the Dedication of the Sonnets by the publisher, Thomas Thorpe, wished an unidentifiable " Mr. W.H. " to enjoy " all happiness and that eternity promised by our ever-living poet ".

The portraits of the Earl of Pembroke show that his hair was dark, whereas that of the addressee in the Sonnets is compared

7

with "buds of marjoram" (Sonnet 99). These might be described as dark auburn—almost a reddish brown. Research has demonstrated that the Sonnets were written from 1594 onwards when Pembroke would have been only 13.

Southampton was eight years older than Pembroke and would not, when 21 years of age, have been addressed as " sweet boy ", especially in a period when men matured much earlier, and even as young as 12 were sent to the Universities. Furthermore, the natures and characters of both candidates do not correspond in any way with that of the " friend ". Against both of these arguments plausible objections are raised at every step, and the whole body of evidence is seen to be merely inferential, and scarcely entitled to be called circumstantial. That the Southampton and Pembroke theories each have their supporters is due to the disposition to accept what is offered rather than be without an identification. Personally, I refuse to accept what cannot be demonstrated.

An equally difficult and controversial problem is that of the so-called " dark lady " (Shakespeare mentions her as " black "). The Pembroke supporters presumed that she was Mary Fitton, the mistress of the Earl. Unfortunately for this argument there happen to be two well-preserved portraits of the lady at Arbury which show her as of fair complexion with brown hair and grey eyes !

The indisputable fact emerges that the Sonnets are auto-biographic and self-revealing. In them Shakespeare creates another self whom he addresses sometimes in the form of a man and sometimes as his own mind or Genius.* For instance, it is plain enough that in the first nineteen Sonnets he is reasoning with himself as to whether he should marry and beget a son in whom his name and memory would survive, or give himself entirely to the creation of heirs of his " invention " which his genius would assure him of immortal fame. That question is decided in Sonnets 18 and 19 in favour of the latter :

My love shall in my verse ever live young.

---

* The late Mr. J. B. Leishman (Senior Lecturer in English Literature at Oxford University) in *Themes and Variations in Shakespeare's Sonnets,* observed that Shakespeare's love for the " friend " is never mentioned as being reciprocated. How strange that such a thought-provoking discovery by a highly intelligent man should not have been questioned as to the reason !

This, of course, does not fit in with the generally accepted view that the man of Stratford was the author of the Sonnets. He had married and had children before he left Stratford. Some Shakespeareans, whose orthodoxy was above suspicion, have questioned the authorship of the Sonnets. They may have done so because the author displays so much knowledge of many different kinds, and shows himself an aristocrat or near-aristocrat. He borrows from Sonnets written by French and Italian authors—Ronsard, Jodell, du Bellay, Desportes and Petrarch's *Laura* especially. To have made himself familiar with those untranslated works could only have been due to private tuition as neither French nor Italian were taught in the schools. There is also proof from the Sonnets that the poet had considerable legal training. He frequently draws upon his forensic knowledge for imagery, and used legal phraseology where there is no occasion to do so. Of Sonnet 46, Lord Campbell, the Lord Chief Justice who wrote *Shakespeare's Legal Acquirements* (1859), said " This Sonnet is so intensely legal in its language and imagery that without a considerable knowledge of English forensic procedure, it cannot be fully understood."

In No. 126 there are curious uses of Exchequer terms within the lines :

> Her audit, though delay'd, answered must be,
> And her quietus is to render thee.

" Quietus " is a technical term for the acquittance which a sheriff receives on settling his accounts at the Exchequer.

No. 134 is full of legal terminology concerning mortgage, and No. 87 has similarly drawn upon the phraseology of conveyances. Note, too, how the word " determination " in its legal meaning of " end " is used in No. 13. " Find no determination " here is equivalent to fee-simple. Nobody but a lawyer would use the word with that meaning. He also frequently illustrates his themes with imagery drawn upon the arts and sciences—music, painting, astronomy, alchemy, medicine and, curiously enough, in no less than four sonnets, distillation. He was, therefore, a man of very considerable culture who had been honoured on some special occasion to walk at the Queen's side, unless the following lines can be made to bear some other meaning :

> Were't aught to me I bore the canopy,
> With my extern the outward honouring,
> Or laid great bases for eternity,
> Which prove more short than waste or ruining?
> Have I not seen dwellers on form and favour
> Lose all, etc.

Certainly, those about the Court would have seen many in favour and great place tumble to disgrace and even the scaffold. I fail to see how the author of the Sonnets could possibly have been the player, nor can the poems be intelligible while the belief that he was is accepted.

I attach significance to the contrasts of light and darkness such as are found in Nos. 33 and 34 :

> Full many a glorious morning have I seen
> Flatter the mountain-tops with sovereign eye,
> Kissing with golden face the meadows green,
> Gilding pale streams with heavenly alchymy ;
> Anon permit the basest clouds to ride
> With ugly rack on his celestial face,
> And from the forlorn world his visage hide,
> Stealing unseen to west with this disgrace :
> Even so my sun one early morn did shine
> With all triumphant splendour on my brow ;
> But out, alack ! he was but one hour mine,
> The region cloud hath mask'd him from me now. . . .

> Why didst thou promise such a beauteous day,
> And make me travel forth without my cloak,
> To let base clouds o'ertake me in my way,
> Hiding thy bravery in their rotten smoke?

He is figuring a personal experience in which fortune and prosperity had smiled upon him early in life but which had now deserted him. The two main groups of Sonnets are addressed to representatives of light and darkness :

> Two loves I have of comfort and despair,
> Which like two spirits do suggest me still,
> The better angel is a man right fair :
> The worser spirit, a woman colour'd ill.
>
> S. 144.

" Suggest " means " tempt " and this is confirmed by what follows :

> To win me soon to hell my female evil
> Tempteth my better angel from my side.

In the pages which follow, I shall endeavour to explain who, or rather what, are personified by the " female evil " and the " better angel " who is called in No. 39 " the better part of me ". Those five words provided the clue which began my quest into the interpretation of the Sonnets.

There is nothing to add to the chapter on " The Rival Poet " included in my " Shakespeare : New Views for Old " (1943) now out of print. Whether one thinks him to have been Drayton, Chapman, or any other of the eight or nine contemporary poets who have been suggested, is not more than an interesting subject for discussion. It does not affect the two main enigmas. I am, however, reproducing the chapter, and also that on the allegorical poem " A Lover's Complaint " which was first printed at the end of the Sonnets in the first edition of 1609, and to which there is a close relationship overlooked by the critics and commentators. There are signs of immaturity in phrasing and style from which it is safe to conclude that it was a composition of Shakespeare's youth. I hope that the revelation as to its inner meaning will rescue the poem from the neglect to which it has been consigned.

It is some fifty years since I first considered the Sonnets apart from their poetry which varies from the sublime to the mediocre. I felt convinced that there must be meanings beneath the surface which had not been revealed. The commentators through the ages had found no satisfactory solution and were divided among themselves. I already had a good knowledge of the Plays and noticed that whenever Fortune was mentioned it was nearly always with bitterness. She was false, fickle, malicious and a wanton. Where such allusions occurred there was nothing in the plot or circumstances to justify such epithets. I noticed, too, that they were all applicable to the " dark lady ". Further study convinced me that she is a personification of Fortune, and as the Sonnets are Shakespeare's self-expression, he had obviously suffered from " the slings and arrows of outrageous fortune ". Many of them show a state of depression and pessimism which is reflected in *Hamlet, Troilus and Cressida, Timon of Athens* and other plays of the middle period in which he turned from comedy to tragedy. His outlook had become serious and gloomy.

The next problem was the identity of the " friend " between whom and the poet a temporary separation had occurred owing to Shakespeare's barren and futile pursuit of the "dark lady". It had led to much unhappiness, and he felt ashamed of himself :

> How have mine eyes out of their spheres been fitted
> In the distraction of this madding fever!
>   S. 119.

and on his penitent return to his "dear Love" promises "mine appetite I never more will grind".

The "friend" is promised immortality through Shakespeare's verse, but as nobody is named, only the poet himself could live in these sonnets. Both Ovid and Horace had expressed their confidence in the imperishable nature of their lines, and it occurred to me that Shakespeare might be following their idea. I remembered having once had to translate the majestic lines with which Ovid ended the 15th and last book of *Metamorphoses,* and returning to it many years later I was greatly impressed by the obvious influence it had upon the mind of Shakespeare. The parallels of thought and expression are too close for coincidence. I give this literal translation :

> And now I have completed a work which neither the anger of Jove, *nor fire, nor sword, nor devouring Time* will be able to destroy. Let that day, which has no power but over my body put an end to my uncertain life when it will. Yet in the better part of me (*parte tamen meliore mei*) I shall be raised immortal above the lofty stars, and indelible shall be my name.

If we consider that Shakespeare is addressing a personification or representation of his own genius, the resemblance with Ovid is apparent :

> Or I shall live your epitaph to make,
> Or you survive when I in earth am rotten ;
> From hence your memory death cannot take,
> Although in me each part will be forgotten.
> *Your name from hence immortal life shall have,*
> *Though I, once gone, to all the world must die :*
> The earth can yield me but a common grave,
> When you entombed in men's eyes shall lie.
> Your monument shall be my gentle verse,
> Which eyes not yet created shall o'er-read.
>   S. 81

There is another echo of Ovid in the middle lines of Sonnet 55 :

> *Nor* Mars his *sword*, *nor* war's quick *fire* shall burn
> The living record of your memory.

" Devouring Time " (*edax vetustas*) occurs at the opening of No. 19.

But to me, the discovery which was far more exciting and important was that Ovid should call his Muse, Mind or Genius " the better part of me ". Years of study have enabled me to memorise the Sonnets pretty well, and twice Shakespeare uses that same phrase for the " friend " addressed, and which I had already suspected was not a contemporary person, but an image created as representative of his poetic genius; the immortal part of him. The first occurs in No. 39 :

> O how thy worth with manners may I sing,
> When thou art all *the better part of me*?
> What can mine own praise to mine own self bring?
> And what is't but mine own when I praise thee?
> Even for this let us divided live,
> And our dear love lose name of *single one*
> That by this separation I may give
> That due to thee which thou deserv'st alone.

The sonnet clearly states that his love is for what he calls, like Ovid, " the better part of me ". For this he promises immortality in one sonnet after another, but he cannot praise it with " manners " (modesty) because, by so doing openly, he would be guilty of self-praise. He, therefore, proceeds to make an imaginary separation between himself and his genius, which he represents as something apart, so that he can express his affection and admiration for his creative work whilst seemingly bestowing it upon another. It is such a thin disguise that I am astonished that none of the learned commentators of several generations has seen through it. In his plays, Shakespeare consistently condemns self-praise, and so does Bacon in his Essay *Of Friendship*.* The Ovidian phrase is repeated in Sonnet 74 :

* Disapproval of self-praise is also expressed in much the same way in *Troilus and Cressida* (I, 3):

> The worthiness of *praise* distains his worth
> If that the prais'd himself bring the praise forth.

Again, in *All's Well* (I, 3): " Then we wound our modesty, and make foul the clearness of our own deservings when, of ourselves, we publish them ". See also the whole of Sonnet 62.

> The earth can have but earth which is his due,
> My spirit is thine, the better part of me.*

The Elizabethan poets were steeped in the classics. Latin was the international language of scholars, and it is not surprising to find that those splendid lines of Ovid inspired others. Thus the poet Daniel calls his Muse his " better part " in *Cleopatra* (594), and Peele in *The Arraignment of Paris* writes :

> And look how much the Mind, the better part,
> Doth overpass the body in desert.

Drayton, in his *Idea* Sonnet 44 declares :

> Ensuing ages yet my rhymes shall cherish
> Where I entombed my better part shall save ;
> And though this earthly body fade and die,
> My name shall mount upon eternity.

The source here seems to have been the last two lines of Ovid's *Amores* :

> Ergo etiam cum me supremis adederit ignis,
> Vivam, parsque mei multa superstes erit.

This is from the same Elegy (Bk. I, 15) as that from which Shakespeare took the two Latin lines placed at the head of *Venus and Adonis*. Ben Jonson, in the first scene of *Poetaster* translates the Latin quotation above as :

> Then when this body falls in funeral fire,
> My name shall live, and my best part aspire.

The relationship between the Mind, Muse or Genius with " the better part ", and its eternal survival, is also to be found in the best known of Horace's *Odes* (Bk. III, 30) beginning " *Exegi monumentum aere perennius* ". It was well-known to Shakespeare for it inspired the opening of Sonnet 55 :

> Not marble, nor the gilded monuments of princes
> Shall outlive this powerful rhyme.

Every educated person of those times would be familiar with the *Odes,* and Shakespeare would remember this particular one :

---

* " Spirit "—The O.E.D. gives the meaning " Incorporeal or immaterial being as opposed to body or matter; Being or intelligence conceived as distinct from, or independent of, anything physical or material " :
What is your substance, whereof are you made?
Sonnet 53.

Non omnis moriar ; multaque pars mei
Vitabit Libitinam,

which may be translated " I shall not wholly die, for the better
part of me shall escape Libitina " (Libitina was the goddess of
Death). Compare also, in the same Ode, what immediately
follows :

usque ego postera
Crescam, laude recens,

(I shall ever be renewed in the praise of posterity)

to the same Sonnet :

Your praise shall still find room
Even in the eyes of all posterity.

Ovid's Epilogue, his Elegy and Horace's Ode are all wholly
concerned with the immortal fame of their verse. The parallels
I have quoted cannot be attributed to chance.

Such were the clues leading to my enquiry and investigation.
I could have wished that somebody, more able than myself, and
one whose name is eminent as a Shakespearean authority, had
undertaken this work which is so long overdue.

I

The Dedication

WHAT a mass of discussion and controversy has raged as to what is meant by the wording, and the strange form of the Dedication of the first edition of the Sonnets in 1609! Many commentators have suggested that the " Mr. W.H." mentioned in it was the person to whom the majority of the Sonnets were addressed. This theory has, however, proved quite unworkable. The manner in which the dedication was printed, being in the shape and form of a monumental inscription, and with full stops after each word, is unique :

TO . THE . ONLIE . BEGETTER . OF .
THESE . INSUING . SONNETS .
Mr. W. H. ALL . HAPPINESSE .
AND . THAT . ETERNITIE .
PROMISED .
BY .
OUR . EVER-LIVING . POET .
WISHETH .
THE . WELL-WISHING .
ADVENTURER . IN .
SETTING .
FORTH .
T.T.

Of the dozen or more persons bearing the initials " W.H.", who have been named for the poet's " beauteous and lovely youth ", only two have received any considerable support, though one of them has the initials reversed. These are William Herbert, Earl of Pembroke, and Henry Wriothesley, Earl of Southampton. There is no evidence that Shakespeare was acquainted with the former, but the two poems *Venus and Adonis* and *The Rape of Lucrece,* published in 1593 and 1594, had been dedicated to the latter. It is, however, absurd to suppose that he would have addressed a peer as " Mr.". Those familiar with the dedications to noblemen have noted the humility in which the authors, if commoners, expressed themselves. The dedications were headed with the full titles of the peers, and ended with the authors', publishers' or printers' expressions of duty and service. A typical example is that of the dedication of the anonymous *The Arte of English Poesie* to Lord Burleigh, signed with the initials of the printer, Richard Field. Throughout it is extremely flattering, and the Lord Treasurer is made out to be a patron of literature and learning, which he was not, for he grudged any encouragement of the arts. The dedication ends with the assurance of the printer being " always ready and desirous to be at your Honourable commandment. And thus I humbly take my leave from the Blackfriars this xxviii of May 1589. Your Honour's most humble at commandment. R.F."

It will be seen, therefore, that Thorpe's dedication bears no resemblance with the style that was employed when a nobleman was addressed. The fact is that there is not the slightest clue as to the identity of " Mr. W.H.". My own guess, which is as good, or as bad, as anybody's, is that he was a friend of the publisher who had procured by some means a scrivener's copy of the sonnets. The book was not printed from the poet's original manuscript for there are too many textual errors which obviously occurred during copying. Thorpe considered that the twelve line verse of Sonnet 126 had the last couplet missing, and left space for it in parentheses. If the manuscript had been handed to him by Shakespeare, Thorpe could have cleared up the matter of the missing two lines. The name " William Shake-speare " (or " Shake-speare ") was a useful one for the piratical printers who evidently knew that it could be used with impunity. The name had already appeared on plays and poems which he certainly did not write. Among those are *The London Prodigal* (1605) and *A Yorkshire Tragedy* (1608); also a book of poems published under the title of *The Passionate Pilgrim* in 1599. Whoever Shakespeare may have been, so far as his literary rights were concerned, he remained " William the Silent ".

II

The Problem of the "Friend"

Sift it as you please, and you shall find
This beauty is the beauty of the Mind.
The Arraignment of Paris (Anon. 1584).

OF the one hundred and fifty-four Sonnets, first printed in
1609, but mainly written some ten to fifteen years earlier,
about 80 are addressed by Shakespeare to his " dear friend ".
The word " friend " is used with a more intimate meaning than
is implied today. The identity of the " beauteous and lovely
youth " has puzzled commentators ever since the first attempt to
match him in some way with one of the poet's contemporaries.
From 1780 onwards, no less than twelve different persons have
been suggested, but only two of them remain. Both Henry
Wriothesley, Earl of Southampton and William Herbert, Earl of
Pembroke, have their supporters, with the former as favourite
because Shakespeare had dedicated the two poems *Venus and
Adonis* (1593) and *The Rape of Lucrece* (1594) to him in
familiar and affectionate terms. Otherwise the arguments
against this theory are insuperable. Plausible objections are
raised at every step, and the whole body of evidence is seen to be
in conflict with that provided in the Sonnets themselves. It is
necessary, in the first place, to remember that class distinctions
were rigorously observed in those days and that players, unless
licensed, were deemed to be " rogues, vagabounds, and sturdye
beggars," and the playhouses were so disreputable in the eyes of
the authorities that they were not allowed within the City
boundaries. In 1595, the Lord Mayor objected to their existence
as near as Shoreditch and Southwark, and he complained to the
Privy Council that " Among other inconveniences it is not the
least that the refuse sort of evil disposed and ungodly people
about this City have opportunity hereby to assemble together and
to make their matches for all their lewd and ungodly practices,

18

being also the ordinary places for all masterless men and vaga-
bond persons to meet together." Two years later the Mayor complained again that the theatres were the haunts of "thieves,
horse-stealers, whoremongers, cozeners, coney-catchers, contrivers
of treason, and other idle and dangerous persons." Even the
festive students of Gray's Inn (after a performance of *The
Comedy of Errors* by the company to which Shakspere was
attached) protested against the insult of having had foisted upon
them "a company of base and common fellows." Like Bacon,
Lord Southampton was at Gray's Inn. The evidence as to the
contemptuous estimation in which actors were held is corro-
borated from many contemporary sources of which the following
from Ben Jonson's *Poetaster* is a fair example :

> *Tucca.* What's he that stalks by there boy?
> 2 *Pyr.* 'Tis a player, Sir.
> *Tucca* A player! call him; call the lousy slave hither;
> what, will he sail by and not once strike or vail to a man of
> war? ha! Do you hear you player, rogue, stalker, come back
> here! (re-enter *Histrio*). No respect to men of worship, you
> slave! what are you proud, ha! you grow rich do you and
> purchase, you twopenny tearmouth?

The "twopenny tearmouth" protests that he saw not the
captain. Further in the scene, as an attraction to the captain,
the player observes :

> We have as much ribaldry in our plays as can be, as you
> would wish, Captain; all the sinners in the suburbs come and
> applaud our action daily.

Acting was not the well-trained and respected profession that
it now is. There were no schools for the teaching of dramatic
art. Players relied on plenty of noise aided by exaggerated
gestures. In the above extract, Ben Jonson calls the player
"stalker". In the play *The Puritain, or the Widow of Watling
Street* (by "W.S." 1607), the question is asked :

> Have you never seen a stalking, stamping player, that will
> raise a tempest with his tongue, and thunder with his heels?

Hamlet's advice to the players is better known :

> It offends me to the soul to hear a robustious periwig-pated
> fellow tear a passion to tatters, to very rags, to split the ears
> of the groundlings, who, for the most part, are capable of
> nothing but inexplicable dumb shows and noise.

It seems complete nonsense to me to imagine that a peer of the realm would be on such intimate terms of affection as existed between the poet and the " friend " of the Sonnets.   In the first nineteen he is urging him to marry and reproduce himself in children :

> Make thee another self for love of me !

Such a liberty taken by a commoner with a peer would have been a Star Chamber offence. The alternative is that Shakespeare is debating with himself, but as the player was already married and had children it could not be him.   Nor was he the son of a widow :

> Is it for fear to wet a widow's eye,
> That thou consum'st thyself in single life?

Bacon's mother had been a widow since 1579, and he himself was unmarried.

Again, the lines are clearly addressed to somebody who was gifted as a poet capable of leaving his name and memory to posterity :

> But wherefore do you not a mightier way,
> Make war upon this bloody tyrant Time?
>   S. 16.

This Sonnet concludes with the significant line :

> And you must live drawn by your own sweet skill.

In the 16th and 17 centuries, " skill " was often used for an art or science.   It could not apply to the begetting of children in which the ignorant are more prolific than the intellectual, and therefore the poet has in mind one who had the skill to beget heirs of the " invention " which, as Shakespeare says, " are begot in the ventricle of memory and delivered upon the mellowing of occasion ".

As instances of this use of the word " skill " one cannot do better than consult Spenser's " Teares of the Muses " in which the Muses lament the low estimation in which they were held :

> The sectaries of my celestial skill
> That wont to be the world's chief ornament.
> My professed skill.
> That secret skill.
> My kindly skill.

Neither Lord Southampton, nor the Earl of Pembroke, nor any other candidate who has been suggested for the " friend ", had the skill to write verse which could defeat " the bloody tyrant Time " in which their name and memory would live. It is Shakespeare himself who, in one Sonnet after another, proudly made claim to that accomplishment :

> You still shall live, such virtue hath my pen.

> So long as men can breathe, or eyes can see,
> So long lives this, and this gives life to thee.

After so many futile attempts to identify the " friend " over the past two hundred years, it should be apparent that some entirely new line of investigation is justified. Professor J. Churton Collins admitted this sixty years ago :

> Unless some fresh discovery is made, nothing new whether in the way of absurdity or sense can be advanced on this subject.

Those words are equally applicable today. If all the scholarship of eminent men-of-letters has failed, it must surely seem futile for one outside that select circle to say anything more on such a very difficult subject. But I cannot bring Southampton, Pembroke, Essex, nor any other supposed patron, within any reasonable distance of being identical with the poet's " beauteous and lovely youth ". *Those who imagine the Sonnets can only be interpreted literally saddle their author with immorality, sexually and homosexually.* For me, they are not addressed to, and do not in the least concern, any other person or object apart from Shakespeare himself. Objection will, perhaps, be raised on the grounds of the familiar reference by Meres in *Palladis Tamia* in 1598 to Shakespeare's " sugred sonnets among his private friends ", but there are no sonnets among those which have come down to us that are in the nature of " sugared sonnets ". They are, for the most part, bitter reflections upon mortality and misfortunes he had endured. Meres alludes to sonnets written in sugared ink so that the writing would shine. These were often sent as compliments between literary gentlemen, and there is an example of one written by John Davies of Hereford in 1610 and addressed :

To the royall, ingenious, and all-learned Knight, Sir Francis Bacon:

> Thy bounty and the Beauty of thy Witt
> Comprised in Lists of Law and learned Arts
> Each making thee for great Imployment fitt
> Which now thou hast (though short of thy deserts),
> Compells my pen to let fall *shining Inke*
> And to bedew the Baies that deck thy Front;
> And to thy health in Helicon to drinke
> As to her Bellamour the Muse is wont:
> For thou dost her embozom; and dost use
> Her company for sport twixt grave affairs;
> So utterest Law the livelyer through thy Muse.
> And for that all thy Notes are sweetest Aires;
>   My Muse thus notes thy worth in ev'ry Line,
>   *With yncke which thus she sugers; so, to shine.*

It would be interesting to know what happened to the products of Bacon's muse. Have his " sweetest Aires " perished, or are they familiar under another name?

Had there been any connection between the Sonnets and a nobleman, such as Southampton, there would surely have been some evidence or tradition about the story of such an infatuation. But Shakespeare's contemporaries apparently knew nothing about it, and the Earl's letters have thrown no light upon the mystery. Were Lord Southampton the addressee, we should expect to find some reference to the promise of a distinguished political and military career. No more acceptable medium of complimenting his " patron " upon the gallantry with which he acquitted himself on the Azores expedition of 1597 (for which he was knighted) could have been desired. But the youth is admired for his " woman's face " and his " woman's gentle heart " (Sonnet 20)—the most inappropriate description of the Earl that could possibly be written.

When John Abraham Heraud in *Shakespeare and his Inner Life* (1865) wrote that after a careful study he had come to the conclusion that " there is not a single Sonnet which is addressed to any individual at all," he came nearer to the truth. If he had added " apart from, or distinct from, the poet's own person and genius," embodying his mind and art, he would have made a great discovery.

In the Sonnets, Shakespeare is soliloquising; treating his genius

or " better part " as a separate being. It is sometimes difficult
to determine when he addresses his own person and when his
poetic muse or genius. In his own words, the problem which
confronts us is :

> One of these men is Genius to the other,
> . . . which is the natural man
> And which the spirit? Who deciphers them?
> > *Comedy of Errors,* V, i.

Both are credited with superlative physical and mental endow-
ments :

> Thou that art now the world's fresh ornament
> And only herald to the gaudy spring.
> > S. 1.

> Shall I compare thee to a summer's day?
> Thou art more lovely and more temperate.
> > S. 18.

> Methinks no face so gracious is as mine,
> No shape so true, no truth of such account ;
> And for myself mine own worth do define,
> As I all other in all worths surmount.
> > S. 62.

> Against that time do I ensconce me here
> Within the knowledge of mine own desert.
> > S. 49.

> You still shall live, such virtue hath my pen.
> > S. 81.

The argument of the first nineteen Sonnets is the respective
advantages of renewing one's image in children, and of dedicat-
ing one's life to the production of works for the benefit of future
ages. It is clear from these Sonnets that the addressee was unmarried and that before the poet, as he writes, is his " painted
counterfeit ". Was it the Hilliard miniature? At least fourteen
portraits of the Earl of Southampton have been identified, but
not one shows him before middle age.

I can no more accept William of Stratford as the writer of
the Sonnets than I can Lord Southampton as the addressee. The
Sonnets are self-revealing. They show the poet as high-born,
accomplished, sensitive, and with an eye and ear for beauty
resplendent with the highest glories of imagination. He draws

upon the arts such as painting, music and poetry. In two of
them (7 and 114) on a courtier's career. There are frequent
similes, metaphors and allusions applied to jewels and apparel.
His indebtedness to French, Italian and Latin poets is too closely
related to be accidental. There are frequent uses of legal terms,
and there are some whole Sonnets written in the language of
law. Examples are Nos. 30, 87 and 134. These are crammed
with images from the laws of inheritance, usury, etc. The
manner in which technical terms and legal processes are pressed
into the service of poetry is ingenious and made to sound quite
natural:

> When to the *sessions* of sweet silent thought
> I *summon* up remembrance of things past,

represents a good example of what I mean. Lord Campbell
in *Shakespeare's Legal Acquirements* (1859) calls particular
attention to Sonnet 46:

> Mine eye and heart are at a mortal war,
> How to divide the conquest of thy sight:
> Mine eye my heart thy picture's sight would bar,
> My heart mine eye the freedom of that right.
> My heart doth plead that thou in him dost lie,
> A closet never pierc'd with crystal eyes,
> But the defendant doth that plea deny,
> And says in him thy fair appearance lies.
> To 'cide this title is impannelled
> A quest of thoughts, all tenants to the heart;
> And by their verdict is determined
> The clear eye's moiety and the dear heart's part,
> As thus; mine eye's due is thine outward part,
> And my heart's right thine inward love of heart.

Lord Chief Justice Campbell, who was writing before the shadow
of the Bacon—Shakespeare controversy had unhappily dimmed
the honesty and perception of commentators, has this to say:

> This sonnet, is so intensely legal in its language and imagery
> that, without a considerable knowledge of English forensic
> procedure, it cannot be fully understood. A lover being
> supposed to have made a *conquest* (i.e. to have gained by
> *purchase*) his mistress, his Eye and his Heart, holding as *joint-
> tenants,* have a contest as to how she is to be partitioned
> between them—each moiety then to be held in severalty.
> There are regular Pleadings in the suit, the Heart being

represented as Plaintiff and the Eye as Defendant. At last issue is joined on what the one affirms and the other denies. Now a jury (in the nature of an inquest) is to be impannelled to 'cide (decide) and by their verdict to apportion between the litigating parties the subject matter to be divided. The jury, fortunately, are unanimous, and, after due deliberation, find for the Eye in respect of the outward form, and for the Heart in respect of the inward love.

Returning to the debate which Shakespeare holds with himself (in Sonnets 1-19) on whether posterity is better provided for by heirs of the " invention " (he calls *Venus and Adonis* " the first heir of my invention ") or in children, the decision is made in Nos. 18 and 19 in favour of the image of the mind :

> But thy eternal summer shall not fade,
> Nor lose possession of that fair (i.e. *beauty*) thou ow'st
> Nor shall Death brag thou wander'st in his shade
> When in eternal lines to time thou grow'st :
>   So long as men can breathe, or eyes can see,
>   So long lives this, and this gives life to thee.

My love shall in my verse ever live young.

This is the argument we find in Bacon's Essay *Of Marriage* :

> Certainly the best works, and of greatest merit for the public, have proceeded from the unmarried or childless men.

Also in the Essay *Of Parents and Children* :

> And surely a man shall see the noblest works and foundations have proceeded from childless men, which have sought to express the images of their minds where those of their bodies have failed ; so the care of posterity is most in those that have no posterity.

In writing thus, Bacon had himself in mind. He considered he was born for the service of mankind, and described himself as the " servant of posterity ", and a similar idea was in the mind of the sonneteer. He might well say, as he does in Sonnet 62 :

> And for myself mine own worth do define,
> As I all other in all worths surmount.

Several sonnets are concerned with the signs of approaching age visible in his looking-glass, and the necessity to make the most use of time :

> Like as the waves make towards the pebbled shore,
> So do our minutes hasten to their end.
>
> S. 60.

Nos. 64 and 65 dwell upon the ruin of monuments, memorials
and buildings in the course of time, whereas the great achieve-
ments of the poet are immortal, and so he resolves to live
eternally by the image of his mind :

> And you must live, drawn by your own sweet skill.
> Yet do thy worst, old Time : despite thy wrong,
> My love shall in my verse ever live young.

Perhaps the most puzzling of all the Sonnets, and one which
has been the cause of more controversy than any other, is the
twentieth :

> A woman's face, with Nature's own hand painted,
> Hast thou, the master-mistress of my passion ;
> A woman's gentle heart, but not acquainted
> With shifting change, as is false woman's fashion ;
> An eye more bright than theirs, less false in rolling,
> Gilding the object whereupon it gazeth ;
> A man in hew, all hews in his controlling,
> Which steals men's eyes and women's souls amazeth.

I cannot understand how anybody who has looked into the
biography of the Earl of Southampton could possibly imagine
that the lines could refer to him. There was nothing womanly
about his face, nor did he have " a woman's gentle heart."
In 1595, he distinguished himself in the tournament given in
honour of the thirty-seventh anniversary of the Queen's
succession. In 1596 and 1597 he joined Essex on two expeditions against the Spaniards off the Azores. In 1600-1, he was
associated with Essex in the rebellion for which Essex was
executed. Southampton was also condemned, but his punish-
ment was commuted to imprisonment for life. He was released
on the accession of King James. Southampton was filled with
martial ardour. He had an impetuous temper, and was often
indulging in court brawls.

The strange being of effeminate nature with the " hew " or
form of a man, with an eye constantly rolling and gilding every
object which he sees, thus amazing " men's eyes and women's
souls ", is undoubtedly Shakespeare's poetic muse personified.

It is " the poet's eye in a fine frenzy rolling ", and turning
the " hews " or forms of things unknown into shapes that are

immortal. That is the description of the poet in *A Midsummer Night's Dream* (V, 1). In *Love's Labour's Lost* we have a description of the philosopher-poet, Biron :

> His eye begets occasion for his wit ;
> For every object that the one doth catch,
> The other turns to a mirth-moving jest,
> Which his fair tongue, conceit's expositor,
> Delivers in such apt and gracious words,
> That *aged ears* play truant at his tales,
> And *younger hearings* are quite ravished ;
> So sweet and voluble is his discourse.
>
> (II, I)

In his *Defence of Poesie,* Sidney tells how the poet comes " with a tale which holdeth *children* from play, and *old men* from the chimney-corner ". Both " Rosaline " in *Love's Labour's Lost,* and Sidney, allude to the persuasive and attractive music of poetry. As the unknown author of *The Arte of English Poesie* (1589) observes, " because it is decked and set out with all manner of colours and figures, which maketh that it sooner inveigleth the judgment of man, and carrieth his opinion this way and that, withersoever the heart by impression of the ear shall be most affectionately bent and directed ". Thus it attracts men and women, young and old. A literal reading of the sonnet would only mean that Shakespeare was a homosexual. An allegorical interpretation puts a different complexion on it. Shakespeare represents the personified genius of poetic art as androgynous, or double-sexed. It refers to the dual character of " eternal love " in the platonic philosophy. The word " passion " was applied in those times to poems. Thomas Watson published in 1582 his *Passionate Century* which consists of 100 sonnets which are called " passions " throughout, and in *A Midsummer Night's Dream* the ditties of Pyramus and Thisbe are so called. Thus the " passion " in this sonnet does not refer to an affair of the heart.*

How could the Earl of Southampton be compared with a treasure belonging to the poet ?—

> Thou best of dearest, and mine only care,
> Art left the prey of every vulgar thief.
> Thee have I not locked up in any chest.

* Bacon in *Wisdom of the Ancients* (Fable XXIV) observes that " every vehement passion appears of a doubtful sex."

Surely Lord Southampton could look after himself! But not so Shakespeare's poetry. Many of his writings are "stolen and surreptitious copies, maimed and deformed by the frauds and stealths of injurious imposters that exposed them", as is stated in the Preface "To the great Variety of Readers" prefixed to the First Folio of the Plays in 1623. Even the name of Shakespeare was placed on the title-pages of plays and poems with which he had no connection.

And how can we possibly apply the lines of Sonnet 53 except as addressed to Shakespeare's own art?—

> What is your substance, whereof are you made,
> That millions of strange shadows on you 'tend?*
> Since every one hath, every one, one shade,
> And you, but one, can every shadow lend.

These shadows, or shapes, attending on the object of the poet's worship are surely identical with the "several strange shapes" which wait upon the command of the "magician" Prospero, who is a later personification of Shakespeare himself. He often uses the word "shapes" to mean an embodiment of fancy, a figure of the imagination. In *Love's Labour's Lost* (IV, 3), poetry is said to be "full of *forms, figures, shapes, objects,* ideas, apprehensions, motions, revolutions. These are begot in the ventricle of memory, nourished in the womb of pia mater, and delivered upon the mellowing of occasion."

The Sonnets are a monument to the poet and his genius, and nobody else has, or can have, any glory in them:

> So long as men can breathe, or eyes can see,
> So long lives this, and this gives life to thee.

Sonnet 124 is also fatal to the Southampton theory, for we are reminded that the poet's "dear love" is not like a mere "child of state". He goes on to declare once again that his love is not subject to the vicissitudes of Time:

> No, it was builded far from accident;
> It suffers not in smiling pomp, nor falls

---

* In Bacon's Masque, *A Conference of Pleasure,* the Hermit who advocates the gifts of the Muses as the most delightful of all recreations, is addressed by his opponent:
"Your mind is of water which taketh all *forms* and impressions, but is *weak of substance.*"
" Impressions " mean ideas or representations.

Under the blow of thralled discontent,
Whereto the inviting time our fashion calls :
It fears not policy, that heretic,
Which works on leases of short-numbered hours,
But all alone stands hugely politic
That it nor grows with heat nor drowns with showers.

It has been suggested, and I think reasonably so, that the poet
had in mind the recent Essex conspiracy which resulted in his
execution and the imprisonment of Southampton.   Those like
Essex and his companions are surely intended by the last couplet
of this sonnet :

To this I witness call the fools of time,
Which die for goodness, who have lived for crime.

One after another those who achieved high office or royal
favour became " the fools of Time " for it was Time which
raised them to the highest dignities, and Time which brought
them to disgrace or the scaffold.

As Shakespeare repudiates any resemblance between his " dear
love "* and " a child of State ", it is further proof that Lord
Southampton, or the like, is not intended.   He alludes to his
mind and art and the children of his " invention ".

Both Francis Bacon and his brother, Anthony, suffered mental
torment over the fall of Essex.   Anthony, who had a delicate
constitution and was always a sick person, died through grief.
Francis was forced by the Queen and Coke to take a part in the
trial of the Earl although he did beg to be excused.

The melancholy of that period is reflected in *Hamlet* and
in some of the sonnets.   Furthermore Bacon was still denied
recognition of his talents and was being kept out of office by
Lord Burleigh and his son, the limping and deformed Robert
Cecil.   In the best-known of Hamlet's soliloquies occur these
lines :

For who would bear the whips and scorns of time,
The oppressor's wrong, the proud man's contumely,
The pangs of despised love, the law's delay,

* J. B. Leishman (Senior Lecturer in English Literature at Oxford
University) in his *Themes and Variations in Shakespeare's Sonnets* (1961)
expressed surprise (p. 226) that nowhere is there evidence that Shakespeare
really believed that his friend " in any deep and meaningful sense of the
word, loved him at all ".   Of course not !   For how can an image of the
mind, devoid of substance, return admiration?

> The insolence of office, and the spurns
> That patient merit of the unworthy takes,
> When he himself might his quietus make, etc.

This hatred of contact with the material world and its corruptions and injustices grates upon the sensitive Shakespeare in Sonnet 66 :

> Tir'd with all these, for restful death I cry,
> As, to behold desert a beggar born,
> And needy nothing trimm'd in jollity,
> And purest faith unhappily forsworn,
> And gilded honour shamefully misplac'd,
> And maiden virtue rudely strumpeted,
> And right perfection wrongfully disgrac'd,
> And strength by limping sway disabled,
> And art made tongue-tied by authority,
> And folly, doctor-like, controlling skill,
> And simple truth miscall'd simplicity,
> And captive good attending captain ill :
>   Tired with all these, from these would I be gone,
>   Save that, to die, I leave my love alone.

The eighth line refers, I think, to the disabling sway of the hunchback, Robert Cecil, over Bacon who, like Hamlet, lacked advancement until the time of James I. Through the influence of his father, the great Lord Burleigh, Robert was appointed to the position of solicitor-general although Bacon was more skilled in law.

The ninth line alludes to the suppression by authority of freedom of opinion in expression or publication. " Art " is commonly used by Shakespeare and Bacon for letters, learning, science, as reference to a Shakespeare Glossary will show. Even the word " artist " meant one skilled in the liberal arts and sciences. Finally, would Shakespeare be likely to speak of " leaving alone " through his death, such a personage as Lord Southampton?

In the group of sonnets from 109-119, occur bitter recollections of an absence from his Muse during which he had been in the public eye and, as he says, " Gor'd mine own thoughts, sold cheap what is most dear ". He regrets the necessity which had forced him into public life and chides Fortune :

> That did not better for my life provide
> Than public means which public manners breed.

His name had received " a brand " and " vulgar scandal " was stamped upon his brow. Twice he mentions " errors " committed during this absence. It cannot be merely a coincidence that Bacon should have written to Sir Thomas Bodley :

> I think no man can more truly say with the psalmist, " multum incola fuit anima mea ", for since I was of any understanding my mind hath in effect been absent from what I have done ; *and in absence are many errors* which I willingly acknowledge ; and among the rest, this great one which led to the rest, that knowing myself by *inward* calling to be fitter to hold a book than to play a part, I have led my life in civil causes, for which I was not very fit by nature, and more unfit by the preoccupation of my mind. Therefore, calling myself home I have now for a time enjoyed my Self, whereof likewise I desire to make the world partaker.

And here is Shakespeare thinking identically :

> O never say that I was false of heart
> Though absence seem'd my flame to qualify ;
> As easy might I from myself depart,
> As from my soul (" anima mea "), which in thy breast doth
> lie
> That is my *home* of love, if I have ranged,
> Like him that travels, I *return* again.
> (S. 109)

> Book both my wilfulness and errors down.
> (117)

> What wretched errors hath my heart committed !
> (119)

> So I return rebuked to my content,
> And gain by ill thrice more than I have spent.
> (119)

Bacon's health was always far from good. As early as 1590, his mother, Lady Anne, wrote to his elder brother, Anthony :

> I verily think your brother's weak stomach to digest hath been much caused and confirmed by untimely going to bed, and then musing *nescio quid* (i.e. I know not what) when he should sleep.

One " coincidence " piles upon another, for there is a confession in Sonnet 27 to the same effect :

> Weary with toil I haste me to my bed,
> The dear repose for limbs with travel tired ;
> But then begins a journey in my head
> To work my mind, when body's work's expired.

I am confident that the reader now has sufficient evidence to reject, as I do, the theory that anybody but " Shakespeare " himself, and the beauty of his own creative mind, are the subjects of these sonnets.

III

The " Dark Lady "

Exeunt Mary Fitton, Lady Penelope Rich, Mistress Davenport,
and Lucy Morgan.

" O, Fortune, Fortune! all men call thee fickle."
Romeo and Juliet (III, 5).

THERE are twenty-five sonnets relating Shakespeare's adventures
with the fickle and false " dark Lady "—a popular title though
Shakespeare does not use it. The series or group begins with
No. 127.

In some of the earlier sonnets, the poet prepares us for that
pessimism which ultimately takes complete possession.

The first indication of the storm is in No. 29, where he
describes himself as an outcast, " in disgrace with Fortune and
men's eyes " :

> When in disgrace with Fortune and men's eyes,
> I all alone beweep my outcast state,
> And trouble deaf heaven with my bootless cries,
> And look upon myself, and curse my fate,
> Wishing me like to one more rich in hope,
> Featur'd like him, like him with friends possess'd,
> Desiring this man's art, and that man's scope,
> With what I most enjoy contented least ;
> Yet in these thoughts myself almost despising,
> Haply I think on thee, and then my state,
> Like to the lark at break of day arising
> From sullen earth, sings hymns at heaven's gate ;
>   For thy sweet love remember'd such wealth brings
>   That then I scorn to change my state with kings.

In the next, he unfolds a tale of many woes, in the
remembrance of which he bewails his " dear time's waste ", and
again consoles himself by turning his thoughts to the love for
his " dear friend " who is the essence of all that is true and

beautiful.   This insubstantial creation of the imagination represents, as I have already shown, his mind, muse or genius, or
" better part " of him.

In No. 37, he again blames Fortune as the cause of all his
sorrow, and repeats that his " friend " is his only comfort :

> So I made lame by Fortune's dearest spite,
> Take all my comfort of thy worth and truth.

The subject is further revived in No. 90, where he says that
he is the object of the world's malice owing to Fortune's spite.
Twice in this sonnet is the word " spite " applied.

Sonnet 110 has been the subject of much commentary, for the
Stratfordians have imagined that there is here an allusion to
detestation of a player's career.   As this sonnet must be coupled
with the one that immediately follows, let us consider the two
together :

> Alas, 'tis true I have gone here and there,
> And made myself a motley to the view,
> Gor'd mine own thoughts, sold cheap what is most dear,
> Made old offences of affections new ;
> Most true it is that I have look'd on truth
> Askance and strangely,

and in self-reproach adds, " Mine appetite I never more will
grind."   The important lines of No. 111 are the first seven :

> O, for my sake do you with Fortune chide,
> The guilty goddess of my harmful deeds,
> That did not better for my life provide
> Than public means which public manners breeds,
> Thence comes it that my name receives a brand,
> And almost thence my nature is subdu'd
> To what it works in, like the dyer's hand.

There is, in fact, no reference here to the profession of player.
Necessity had compelled him to seek a living in the material
world apart from the artistic which he loved, and for which he
considered himself eminently fitted.   In Bacon's case it was the
law which he said was distasteful to him and for which, he
confessed, " I am unfit by the preoccupation of my mind."
The word " public " is used in the Latin meaning of " *publicus* "
(appertaining to the State).   Thus in *As You Like It* (I, 3) " our
public court ", " public laws " (*Timon of Athens,* V. 5).   It is

so used today in the titles of State institutions, offices and
officials. The word " public " in Sonnet 111 does *not* allude
to the playhouse or the audiences.

Shakespeare continues to chide Fortune in a number of other
sonnets leading up to the " dark lady " group.

Now there is no doubt in my mind that he borrowed his
treatment of the subject from Chaucer's poems, particularly
The Romaunt of the Rose :

> Another love also there is,
> That is contrarie unto this,
> Which desyre is so constreyned,
> That it is but while feyned ;
> Awey fro trouthe it doth so varie,
> That to good love it is contrarie.
> This love cometh of dame Fortune,
> That little while wol contune ;
> For it shall chaungen wonder soon,
> And take eclips right as the moon.

Similarly the device of the " dark lady ", and the other allusions
to the evil influence of the pursuit of Fortune, are but instances
of " dressing old words new " (76). In Chaucer's allegorical
poem of the search for the Rose (the emblem of Truth and
Beauty) in which Dame Fortune, like an evil spirit, tempts the
seeker astray, " Reason " defines true friendship, and contrasts
its benefits with the ills into which men run by pursuing Fortune.
As in the Sonnets, there is insistence upon her frowardness,
mutability, perverseness and wantonness :

> For this Fortune that I of telle,
> With men whan hir lust to dwelle,
> Makith hem to lese her conisaunce,
> And nourishith hem in ignoraunce.

Dame Reason also gives a long sermon upon the various kinds
and degrees of love. Reason is the physician, as these lines,
spoken by the sufferer from the " disease " plainly show :

> Thus as I made my passage
> In compleynt, and in cruel rage,
> And I nist where to find a leche
> That couthe unto myn helping eche,
> Out of her tour I saugh Resoun,
> Discrete and wys, and ful pleasaunt,
> And of her porte ful avenaunt.

Later on, we learn that the counsel and prescriptions of Reason were ignored. In Sonnet 147, Reason is again the physician and, as Chaucer wrote, " her doctrine sette at nought " :

> My love is as a fever longing still
> For that which longer nurseth the disease ;
> Feeding on that which doth preserve the ill,
> Th' uncertain-sickly appetite to please.
> My reason, the physician to my love,
> Angry that his prescriptions are not kept,
> Hath left me.

Chaucer makes Reason commend such love as that of friendship :

> Love there is in sondry wyse,
> As I shall thee here devyse.
> For some love leful is and good ;
> I mean not that which makith thee wood (i.e. *mad*)
> And ravisshith from thee all thy wit,

which Shakespeare transmutes in the lines :

> Past cure I am now Reason is past care,
> And frantic *mad* with evermore unrest ;
> My thoughts and my discourse as madmen's are,
> At random from the truth vainly expressed.

Chaucer then makes Reason give a warning against lustful love, and also love of Fortune as certain to disqualify him who seeks :

> For to gete and have the Rose.

The Rose, as I have mentioned, is the emblem of Truth and Beauty as applied to the soul :

> O, how much more doth *beauty* beauteous seem
> By that sweet *ornament* which truth doth give !
> The rose looks fair, but fairer we it deem
> For that sweet odour which doth in it live.
>
> (54)

Compare this with Bacon in a letter to the Earl of Rutland in 1595, " The greatest *ornament* is the inward *beauty of the mind* ". " Truth " has the meaning of reason and knowledge, and the Roman philosophers called her " the daughter of Time ", and the glory of Time is to bring forth Truth, and so

Shakespeare proudly boasts that his genius will live in his verse
" so long as men can breathe or eyes can see ". The poet's
mind is obsessed with this thought for it is his all in all :

> For nothing this wide universe I call.
> Save thou, my *Rose,* in it thou art my all.
>
> (109)

It is the " Rose " of Chaucer's poem, and the " eternal rose " of
Dante (*Paradiso* XXX).

A considerable portion of Chaucer's *Book of the Duchesse*
is also devoted to a discussion concerning the evil deeds of
Fortune :

> To *derke* is turned all my light,
> My wit to foly, my day is night,
> My love is hate, my sleep waking, etc.

which Shakespeare turns into :

> Love is my sin, and my dear virtue hate ;
> Hate of my sin, grounded on sinful loving.

Chaucer's association of the malevolence and fickleness of
Fortune with night and darkness is significant.

The famous " dark lady " is, I find, merely a personification
of Fortune. The poet is careful to explain that she is only
imagined, and pictured as dark, because of her deeds :

> In nothing art thou black, save in thy *deeds,**
> And thence this slander, as I think, proceeds.

Bacon wrote that " Fortune is not content to do a man one ill
turn ".

Shakespeare sees the " dark lady " as an abhorrence. He has
been betrayed by her but, in spite of everything, his heart still
loves what his eyes despise. The references to her beauty or
otherwise are frequently contradictory. In one sonnet he writes
of her as one " whose beauties proudly make her cruel ", but
later on says :

> My mistress' eyes are nothing like the sun ;
> Coral is far more red than her lips' red ;
> If snow be white, why then her breasts are dun,

---

* The Romans used " niger " (*black*) for bad, unlucky or ill-omened (see
e.g. Horace, *Satires* I. ix). Shakespeare has " black despair ", " black
tidings," etc. Caliban is " a thing of darkness ".

> If hairs be wires, black wires grow on her head.
> I have seen roses damask'd red and white,
> But no such roses see I in her cheeks.
>
> (S. 130)

These descriptions are altogether so inconsistent that it is plain some shape of the poetic imagination was the subject.

Certainly, Fortune was, one way and another, Bacon's "worser spirit", as Shakespeare calls her in that sonnet beginning "Two loves I have of comfort and despair" (144).

In his birth and upbringing she was his friend, but abandoned him almost to beggary on the death of his father, Sir Nicholas Bacon, when Francis, who was the youngest of six sons, was only eighteen. His share, under his father's will, was negligible and his tastes were extravagant. He entered with zest into the gay and lavish society at Gray's Inn, becoming treasurer of the Inn, and providing for the revels and entertainments out of his own pocket. He lacked advancement during Elizabeth's reign, being kept out of office by Burleigh who naturally promoted his son, Robert Cecil, to the offices which would otherwise have gone to Bacon. Necessity compelled him to employ his intellect and his facile pen in other matters which occupied time which he would rather have devoted to philosophy and the muses. He, and his brother Anthony, were in the service of the Earl of Essex in political and secret service work. Many letters written by Essex to the Queen were, in fact, written on his behalf by Bacon and, though bearing Essex's signature, the style is unmistakable.

Shakespeare's allusions to Fortune are generally very bitter. She is unkind, fickle and a wanton, and all these vices are combined in the "dark lady" :

> O, call me not to justify the wrong,
> That thy unkindness lays upon my heart
>
>   Those lips of thine,
> That have profaned their scarlet ornaments,
> And seal'd false bonds of love as oft as mine.

That the temptation of Fortune had interfered with his Muse and studies is clear from this sonnet :

> To win me soon to *hell* my female evil,
> Tempteth my better angel from my side,
>
> (144)

Darkness is associated with *hell* in *Love's Labour's Lost* (IV, 3) :

> Black is the badge of hell,

Also in *King Lear* (IV, 6) :

> There's hell : there's darkness.

In *Troilus and Cressida*, Shakespeare observes that " some men creep in skittish Fortune's hall, while others play the idiot in her eyes ". One of Bacon's aphorisms is, " Fortune makes him a fool whom she makes her darling," and this is exactly what happens to the writer of the Sonnets :

> Be it lawful I love thee, as thou lov'st those
> Whom thine eyes woo as mine importune thee :
> Root pity in thy heart that when it grows,
> Thy pity may deserve to pitied be.

In *Hamlet,* he says " blessed are they whose blood and judgment are so well commingled, they are not a pipe for Fortune's finger to sound what stop she please ". In Sonnet 128, he pictures his " mistress " playing, not the pipe (for that would destroy the illusion) but the virginals. The " Jacks " which, he says, " leap to kiss the tender inward of her hand " signify those men whose ambitions are fixed upon securing the favours of Fortune. " Jack " means any contemptible person—" silken, sly, insinuating jacks " (*Richard III*), and elsewhere in the Plays. When Shakespeare makes her play upon those " saucy jacks ", and begs her to " give them thy fingers, me thy lips to kiss ", he makes a technical error which, I think, was committed wilfully for the sake of punning upon " jacks ". His knowledge of music has been proved to be complete and accurate, and he would have known that the *keys,* and not the jacks, were fingered in playing the virginals. The strings were plucked by quills which were secured to the jacks, and which in turn were set in motion by the keys.

Shakespeare has pursued Fortune feverishly only to find him-self " her neglected child " (143). Now this is significant for we often talk of " a child of Fortune " (*Fortunae filius*), which is an expression derived from Horace. The term would hardly be appropriate if the poet was writing of a real mistress. He declares that he can gain no " fair acceptance " with her, but he cannot turn back.   He might say with poor mad Lear, " I am even the natural fool of Fortune " :

> But my five wits, nor my five senses can,
> Dissuade one *foolish* heart from serving thee,*
> Who leaves unsway'd the likeness of a man,
> Thy proud heart's slave, and vassal wretch to be.

For this devotion he has only met with " Fortune's buffets " and not with her rewards—" She that makes me sin awards me pain ".   Other attributes of Fortune mentioned in the Plays are blindness and inconstancy :

> That goddess blind . . . she is turning and inconstant.
> *Henry V,* (III, 6).

We find all the vices and defects of Fortune, as mentioned in the plays, combined in the " dark lady " :

> I am perjur'd most,
> For all my vows are oaths, but to misuse thee,
> And all my honest faith in thee is lost ;
> For I have sworn deep oaths of thy deep kindness,
> Oaths of thy love, thy truth, thy constancy ;
> And, to enlighten thee, gave eyes to *blindness*
> Or made them swear *against* the thing they see.
> For I have sworn thee fair, more perjur'd I
> To swear against the truth, so foul a lie.
> (152)

Other " good set terms " with which Shakespeare railed against Lady Fortune, and which are applicable to the " dark lady " are :

> The malevolence of Fortune.
> Fortune's malice.
> Fortune's spite.
> Crooked Fortune.
>   (In S. 151, the " dark lady " is a " cheater ".)
> Fortune's fickleness.
> Chiding Fortune.
> I am the most disdained of Fortune.
> He's but Fortune's knave, a minister to her will.
> Dark as your fortune.

These and other imprecations occur as reference to a Shakespeare concordance will show.

---

* " *Fortuna, nimium quem fovet, stultum facit* " (*Publius Syrus*)— " Fortune makes a fool of the man whom she caresses too much."

In Sonnet No. 143, Shakespeare compares her to a " *House-wife* " running to catch one of her feathered creatures which has broken away, and he sees himself as " her neglected child " who " holds her in chase " and who :

> Cries to catch her whose busy care is bent
> To follow that which flies before her face,
> Not prizing her poor infant's discontent;
> So runn'st thou after that which flies from thee,
> Whilst I, thy babe, chase thee *afar behind*.

Bacon draws a similar analogy of Fortune as a woman elusive in pursuit. It occurs in *The Advancement of Learning* (Book II) :

> It is not amiss for men, in their race toward their fortune, to cool themselves a little with that conceit which is elegantly expressed by the Emperor Charles V, that Fortune has somewhat of the nature of a woman who, if she be too much wooed, is commonly *the further off*.

There were two different meanings to the word " housewife ", and one of them, now obsolete, meant a jilt, strumpet or hussy. In the first edition of the Sonnets, the word is printed " huswife ", and Shakespeare is playing upon the two meanings as he does with " jacks ".

In the plays we have :

> " The housewife Fortune."   (*As You Like It.*)
> " The false housewife Fortune."   (*Antony and Cleopatra.*)
> " Doth Fortune play the housewife with me now? "
> > (*Henry V.*)

Bianca, the courtesan, is :
> " A housewife that by selling her desires
> Buys herself bread and clothes." (*Othello*)

Bacon believed that he was born for the service of mankind and, to that end had taken all knowledge to be his province. Worldly ambition had, however, temporarily enticed his " better angel " from his side, and he had given to mundane affairs time and consideration which, he considered, should have been devoted to the lasting good of all men.

The Sonnets inform us that Shakespeare sought, in his writings, no personal gain or glory. His mind was fixed upon posterity. " Enough for me," wrote Bacon, " the consciousness of well-deserving and those real and effectual results with which Fortune cannot interfere ". (*Proem* to *Great Instauration.*)

IV

The Rival Poet

IT is difficult to realise that in his own time, and for a century
after his death, nobody had any suspicion that the genius of
Shakespeare was unique, and that those who ranked him highly
as an author compared him with Spenser, Sidney, Drayton,
Chapman and even lesser lights, and that most of the judges of
that time assigned the first place to one of them. We merely
find the iteration of the same vapid and affected compliments,
couched in conventional terms, comparing Shakespeare's
" tongue ", pen or vein, to silver, honey, sugar or nectar, while
they ignore his greater and distinguishing qualities. It was not
until well into the 18th century that Shakespeare's literary fame
really began. Such of his plays as had been presented had been
mutilated and " improved " almost beyond recognition. From
1623 to 1685 only four complete editions of his plays were
published, and from 1609 to 1710, only one edition of the
Sonnets intervened, and that was of a selected number with
fancy headings put to them.

Although comparatively unappreciated in his own time,
Shakespeare knew that he stood alone in his sphere. In his own
words :

I all other in all worths surmount.

(S. 62)

In the Sonnets, Shakespeare has given us his own opinion of
his genius. He knew quite well that his profound reach of
thought, and his unrivalled knowledge of human nature, were
beyond the vulgar ken, as were the higher graces of his poetry.
That, at least, is made clear in the Sonnets.

It is natural, therefore, that he should have been susceptible
to contemporary criticism, and to being so little valued by the
men of his age. It is scarcely surprising, too, that he should
express his disappointment that other poets should have been

42

held in even higher esteem. There are nine sonnets (Nos. 78-86) which allude to one particular rival poet.

His identity has been claimed for several different poets of the period, and the name of George Chapman has, so far, been the most popular of the guesses. The case for Chapman depends upon Shakespeare's " beauteous and lovely youth " having been a patron, and then connecting that patron with both Chapman and Shakespeare. It has been assumed, without the slightest warrant for doing so, that Chapman sought the patronage of Lord Southampton for his early poems (1594 5) and was rejected. Chapman had produced no conspicuously great verse until he began his translation of Homer in 1598. In 1610, the complete edition appeared, and a series of sixteen sonnets was appended, one of which was addressed to Southampton. But Shakespeare's Sonnets were printed in 1609, and were obviously written some years earlier, whilst Chapman's sonnet was couched in terms of formality, and the writer implied that he had had no previous close connection with the distinguished nobleman.

There is nothing in common between the gifts and style of Shakespeare and Chapman, and Shakespeare's judgment would have been too sound for him to refer to Chapman as a " worthier pen ", who wrote :

> In polished form of well-refined pen,

or to have humbled himself before a craftsman of such inferior merit in this strain :

> My tongue-tied Muse in manners holds her still,
> Whilst comments of your praise, richly compiled,
> Reserve their character with golden quill
> And precious phrase by all the Muses filed.

> I am a worthless boat,
> He of tall building and of goodly pride.

Although falling in with the prevailing fashion Shakespeare does not seem to have been very happy writing in the Sonnet form. Its regularity, and the management of the rhymes, are troublesome, and the expression of thought is necessarily cramped and confined. It is in the high-flying conceits and the grander music of blank verse that Shakespeare's " golden cadence " is unsurpassed. He was not ignorant of this fact, and expressed

his regret that in writing sonnets his " poor rude lines " do not
keep pace with " the bettering of the time " (32), and that in
this form of verse, his Muse had not " grown with this growing
age ".   It must be admitted that the *best* of Drayton's sonnets
are superior in form, finish and poetical merit to several of those
published as Shakespeare's.   Although he was presumably aware
of this, he could at least claim distinction in his choice of theme.
He dissociates himself from the sonneteers who spend their
might in extravagant praise of their real or imaginary mistresses :

> So is it not with me as with that Muse
> Stirr'd by a painted beauty to his verse,
> Who heaven itself for ornament doth use
> And every fair with his fair doth rehearse,
> Making a couplement of proud compare,
> With sun and moon, and earth and sea's rich gems.
>
> (S. 21)

In his " Idea "* sonnets, Drayton, like Shakespeare, denies
that his lines are inspired by passion.   To the 1599, and all
later editions, he prefixed the following lines : " To the Reader
of these Sonnets," which might equally well apply to Shakespeare's.   It is curious that the key to the interpretation of the
latter suggested by Drayton's Preface has been overlooked :

> Into these lines, who but for passion looks
> At this first sight, here let him lay them by,
> And seek elsewhere in turning others' books
> Which better may his labour satisfy !
> No far-fetched sigh shall ever wound my breast !
> Love from mine eyes a tear shall never wring :
> No *Ah-mes* my whining sonnets drest !
> A libertine ! fantasticly I sing !
> My verse is the true image of my mind,
> Ever in motion still desiring change. . . .
> > My muse is rightly of the English strain,
> > That cannot long one fashion entertain.

In the sonnets which follow, Drayton, like Shakespeare,
addresses his poetic Muse in remarkably similar terms, but with
the difference that Drayton is undisguised, and he has warned

* Drayton uses " Idea " in its original classical meaning of an image or
representation, as does Shakespeare in *Richard III* (III, 7):

> Withal I did infer your lineaments,
> Being the right idea of your father,
> Both in your form and nobleness.

his readers not to look for " passion ". He writes with all the Shakespearean confidence in the immortality of his verse.

Generally speaking, the critics seem to have accepted the theory that Chapman was the rival poet, not because the evidence on his behalf is strong, but from the disposition to accept what is offered rather than be without an identification. If the same amount of labour had been spent in considering the claims of Drayton, it would have been agreed that there are firmer grounds here, and evidence that cannot be easily assailed.

In Sonnet 78, Shakespeare tells us that whatever he writes he is indebted to the assistance or inspiration of the " friend " :

> Yet be most proud of that which I compile
> Whose influence is thine, and born of thee.

We next learn that he has enjoyed a monopoly of that influence but now there is another claiming it :

> Whilst I alone did call upon thy aid,
> My verse alone had all thy gentle grace ;
> But now my gracious numbers are decay'd.
> And my sick muse doth give another place.

I discovered the first clue to his identity in Sonnet 80 :

> Knowing a better spirit doth use your name,
> And in the *praise* thereof *spends all his might*.

There is an echo here from Drayton's " dedicated lines " addressed to the Countess of Bedford and prefixed to *Endimion and Phoebe* (1594)—a rival poem to Shakespeare's *Venus and Adonis,* which had been printed in the previous year. Drayton has :

> Upon whose *praise* my soul shall *spend her might*.

The parallelism is too close to be accidental.

The most difficult point of contact between any claimant for the rival poet, and Shakespeare's obscurely-worded references, is Sonnet 86. Who could it have been whose " spirit " was " by spirits taught to write above a mortal pitch ? " And what is meant by the " compeers by night, giving him aid ? " :

> Was it his spirit, by spirits taught to write
> Above a mortal pitch, that struck me dead ?
> No, neither he nor his compeers by night

Giving him aid, my verse astonished.
He, nor that affable familiar ghost
Which nightly gulls him with intelligence,
As victors of my silence cannot boast,
I was not sick of any fear from thence.
But when your countenance fil'd up his line,
Then lack'd I matter; that enfeebled mine.

The answer is to be found in Drayton's great poem *The Barons'
Wars*, in which he twice appeals for supernatural aid to guide
his enterprise. The first is in Canto I, 4:

O Thou, the wise director of my Muse,
Upon whose bounty all my powers depend,
Into my breast thy sacred'st fire infuse;
Ravish my spirit this great work to attend:
Let the still *night* my laboured lines peruse
That when my poems gain their wished end,
Such whose sad eyes shall read this tragic story,
In my weak hand may see Thy might and glory.

The other is in Canto IV, 39, where Drayton, about to relate
" new sorts of plagues . . . strange apparitions and prodigious
birth, unheard-of sickness and calamities ", writes:

Now lighter humour leave me and be gone,
Your passion poor yields matter much too slight;
To write those plagues that then were coming on,
Doth ask a pen of ebon and the *night*.
If there be ghosts their murder that bemoan,
Let them approach me, and in piteous plight
Howl, and about me with black tapers stand
To lend a sad light to my sadder hand.

Meres, in *Palladis Tamia* (1598), reports that Drayton is
termed " golden-mouthed, for the purity and preciousness of his
style ", and in Guilpin's *Skialetheia*, printed in the same year,
it is stated again that " Drayton is justly surnamed golden-
mouthed ".

In his *Satire* VI, Guilpin names seven representative English
poets. They are Chaucer, Gower, Spenser, Daniel, Markham,
Drayton and Sidney. Shakespeare is not mentioned! Just as
Meres says that Drayton is called " golden-mouthed " and refers
to the " preciousness of his style ", so Shakespeare writes of the
rival's " golden quill " and his " precious phrase ".

The main theme of both the Shakespeare and the Drayton

sonnets is very similar in that both praise their own art while
seemingly bestowing it upon an individual; and the turns of
speech employed by the respective authors are so alike that there
must have been some unsuspected connection between them.
For instance, Drayton's Sonnet 44 would not have been out of
place among the Shakespeare collection:

> Whilst thus my pen strives to eternize thee,
> Age rules my lines with wrinkles in my face,
> Where, in the map of all my misery,
> Is modelled out the world of my disgrace;
> Whilst in despite of tyrannizing times,
> Medea-like, I make thee young again,
> Proudly thou scorn'st my world out-wearing rhymes
> And murderest Virtue with thy coy disdain:
> And though in youth my youth untimely perish,
> To keep thee from oblivion and the grave,
> Ensuing ages yet my rhymes shall cherish,
> Where I entombed *my better part* shall save;
>> And though this earthly body fade and die,
>> My name shall mount upon eternity.

Like Shakespeare's, Drayton's sonnets bear many traces of
Ovidian inspiration. One cannot help noticing here, particularly
in the concluding couplet the debt to Ovid's *Amores*, Book I,
Elegy 15, the last lines of which—as translated by Ben Jonson
—read:

> Then when this body falls in funeral fire,
> My name shall live, and my best part aspire.

Compare the first line of Drayton's sonnet with:

> You still shall live, such virtue hath my pen.
>> (81)

Line 2 with:

> Against my love shall be as I am now,
> With Time's injurious hand crush'd and o'erworn:
> When hours have drained his blood, and fill'd his brow
> With lines and wrinkles.
>> (63)

Line 6 with:

> Painting my age with beauty of thy days.
>> (62)

The " tyrannising times " of Drayton are the subject of Shakespeare's Sonnet 66, while we meet the sentiments of the last six
lines of Drayton's in Shakespeare's No. 18 :

> But thy eternal summer shall not fade,
> Nor lose possession of that fair thou ow'st,
> Nor shall death brag thou wander'st in his shade,
> When in eternal lines to time thou grow'st.
>   So long as men can breathe, or eyes can see,
>   So long lives this, and this gives life to thee.

Drayton's reference to his " Idea " as " my better part " is, of
course, Shakespeare's expression (derived from Ovid) for his Art
in Sonnet 39 :

> O, how thy worth with manners may I sing,
> When thou art all the better part of me?

Drayton was a poet of the same " School " as Shakespeare.
That is to say, his poetry was of the highly imaginative or
fanciful vein.   Both refer to poetry as the fruit of " invention ",
for as *Venus and Adonis* was called " the first heir of my
invention ", so Drayton writes :

> When I, as fast as e'er my pen could trot
> Pour'd out what first from quick invention came,
> Nor never stood one word thereof to blot.

He then claims to have mounted Heaven for phrase, and to have
" ransacked all Apollo's golden treasury " for terms in which to
sing the praises of his fair " Idea ".   I am sure it was this
extravagant but superbly worded claim in Drayton's 21st sonnet
which made Shakespeare allude to the " precious phrase by all
the Muses fil'd " (i.e. *polished*) with which his rival wrote.
There were good reasons for Drayton being regarded as a rival
in bringing forth hyperbolical rhetoric for the praise of his
immortal part.

Drayton's Sonnet 16 is headed " An Allusion to the Phoenix ",
and in it he proclaims his " Idea " as the Phoenix.   Now there
can be only *one* Phoenix and Drayton, having published that
sonnet in 1594, had claimed it first, and other sonneteers would
be compelled to ransack their brains for other worthy com-
parisons for " the immediate jewel of their souls ".   The concluding lines of that sonnet read :

Yourself thus burned in that sacred flame,
With so rare sweetness all the heavens perfuming,
Again increasing as you are consuming,
Only by dying born the very same ;
    And winged by fame you to the stars ascend,
    So you of time shall live beyond the end.

Shakespeare's Sonnets 83 and 84 appear to have been written in allusion to this, for the Phoenix consumed herself in her ashes to rise again. This, I think, is the " tomb " mentioned in these lines :

How far a modern quill doth come too short,
Speaking of worth what worth in you doth grow!
This silence for my sin you did impute,
Which shall be most my glory, being dumb,
For I impair not beauty being mute,
When others would give life, and bring a tomb.
    There lives more life in one of your fair eyes
    Than both your poets can in praise devise.

Who is it says most? which can say more,
Than this rich praise, that you alone are you?
In whose confine immured is the store
Which should example where your equal grew.

The parallelisms between the Sonnets of these two writers are so numerous that to treat them at length is impossible here. I will, however, point out an instance of more than ordinary significance because it shows how the thoughts of Shakespeare and Drayton were pursuing the same end and running in the same channel.

Shakespeare writes (38) :

For who's so dumb that cannot write to thee,
When thou thyself dost give Invention light?
Be thou the tenth Muse, ten times more in worth
Than those old nine which rhymers invocate!
    And he that calls on thee, let him bring forth
    Eternal numbers to outlive long date.

Drayton also thought *his* " better angel " was worthy of being the " tenth Muse ", and as his Sonnet was first printed in 1594, he anticipated Shakespeare :

Nine worthy women to the world were given
My worthy one to these nine worthies addeth,
And my fair Muse, one Muse unto the nine,

D

And my good angel, in my soul divine,*
With one more order these nine orders gladdeth.
My Muse, my worthy, and my angel then,
Makes every one of these three nines a ten.

It can certainly be said that Drayton wrote " in polished form
of well-refined pen " (85). Fuller, who was twenty-three when
Drayton died, described him as " a pious poet, his conscience
having always the command of his fancy; very temperate in his
life, slow of speech and inoffensive in company ". Barnfield, in
1598, paid a very high tribute to him, placing him as inferior
to none of his contemporaries :

And Drayton whose well-written tragedies
And sweet epistles soar thy fame to skies;
Thy learned name is equal with the rest
Whose stately numbers are so well addressed.

The broad towering metre of Drayton's *Harmonie of the
Church* justifies Shakespeare's reference to " the proud full sail
of his great verse ". The poem was printed in 1591 and consists
of " Hymns ". Can it be yet another coincidence that in Sonnet
85, Shakespeare says that he cries " Amen " to " every hymn
that able spirit affords " ?

Shakespeare's allusion to " the dedicated words which writers
use, of their fair subject *blessing* every book ", is particularly apt
if Drayton was the rival poet. In the *Heroical Epistles* there
are 11 books and 11 inscriptions—one " blessing " for each
division of the work—to Lady Harrington, the Earl and Countess
of Bedford, etc. The first three books of *Polyolbion* are introduced with dedicatory flourishes.

Among those poets who, under the veil of love sonnets, sang
the beauty of their minds, or " Knowledge, the wing wherewith
we fly to heaven " (Poesy, perhaps, being the other wing)
Drayton comes nearest to Shakespeare and will, I feel sure, be
accepted as the rival poet.

---

* " *My fair Muse . . . my good angel.*" Compare Shakespeare S.144.
" My better angel is a man right fair." " Angel " is used in the meaning of
genius, daemon or *spirit.*

V

Shakespeare At Bath!

THE last two Sonnets (Nos. 153 and 154) are versions of a
Greek epigram by the Byzantine, Marianus, probably of the
5th century. The original source of this pair of Sonnets was
the *Palatine Anthology*, Bk. ix, No. 637. There was no English
translation, but one in Latin was included in *Selecta Epigram-
mata*, printed at Basel in 1529, and in some other collections
of epigrams before the end of that century. There is a translation in Mackail's *Epigrams from the Greek Anthology*, 1890,
p. 191. Before discussing Shakespeare's adaptation and
embellishment of the epigram, it is helpful to quote Sonnet 154
which begins thus:

> The little Love-god lying once asleep
> Laid by his side his heart-inflaming brand,
> Whilst many nymphs that vow'd chaste life to keep
> Came tripping by: but in her maiden hand
> The fairest votary took up that fire
> Which many legions of true hearts had warm'd;
> And so the general of hot desire
> Was sleeping by a virgin hand disarm'd.

In the Greek original, the slumbering Love gives his torch
to the nymphs' keeping, and they, to quench it, dip it into the
waters, but the torch kindles the waters, and "the amorous
nymphs pour hot water thence into the bathing pool". In
Shakespeare's version it is not "amorous nymphs", but "nymphs
that vowed *chaste* life to keep", and not the nymphs generally,
but *one* of them that is said to take up the "heart-inflaming
brand". This nymph is described as "the fairest votary", and
in the companion sonnet (No. 153) is called "a maid of Dian's".
Why this alteration? And to whom does it allude? There can
be no doubt that this "fairest votary" is the same as "the
imperial votaress" of *A Midsummer Night's Dream*, against
whom Cupid's "fiery shaft" was launched in vain, being

" quench'd in the chaste beams of the watery moon "; and we
are reminded of the famous portrait of Queen Elizabeth as
Diana with the crescent moon on her brow.

In Sonnet 153 this " maid of Dian's " steeps the " love-
kindling fire ",

> In a cold valley-fountain of that ground ;
> Which borrowed from this holy fire of Love
> A dateless lively heat, still to endure,
> And grew a seething *bath,* which men yet prove
> Against strange maladies a sovereign cure.
> But at my mistress' eye Love's brand new-fired,
> The boy for trial needs would touch my breast ;
> I, sick withal, the help of bath desired,
> And thither hied, a sad distempered guest,
> But found no cure.

There may be an allusion here to the ever warm medicinal
waters of Bath, and the city which lies in a valley. Thither the
poet hied " a sad distempered guest ". As there can be no
doubt but that the " maid of Dian's " (153), and " the fairest
votary " (154) refer to Queen Elizabeth, it is reasonable to
conclude that he went to Bath as one of her retinue. Although
the poet " found no cure " for his distemperature (whatever that
may have been), the Queen apparently benefited as the water
proved " a sovereign cure ".

She visited Bath in 1592 and was entertained at the nearby
country seat of her godson, Sir John Harrington. There may
have been other visits by her which have not been recorded.
The Greek epigram does not mention the word " bath ", but
merely " bathing-pool " which is not credited with curative
powers.

It is impossible to believe that the composer of these two
supplementary sonnets was not the same as of the others.

Whoever the author of Sonnets 153 and 154 may have been,
it is clear that he was a person of some social status to have
visited the Spa as a " guest " on a royal visit, and that he was
in need of cure. He was a scholar whose reading extended to
the lesser-known classics. It seems to me that there was nobody
of that period fulfilling these requirements better than Bacon.
His health from infancy had been far from good and he was
constantly resorting to medicines. He considered that his

infirmities were due to his father, Sir Nicholas, having been elderly, obese and gouty. He was the youngest of six sons, four of whom were by the first wife. Both Anthony and Francis, the two sons of Lady Anne, had poor health. The account-book of Dr. Whitgift, their tutor at Trinity College, Cambridge, mentions their sicknesses and the money he spent on medicines for them.

In 1590, their mother wrote to Anthony :

> I verily think your brother's weak stomach to digest hath been much caused and confirmed by untimely going to bed, and then musing *nescio quid* when he should sleep.

If it be a coincidence, it is, indeed, a strange one that the poet in Sonnet 27 should write to the same effect :

> Weary with toil I haste me to my bed,
> The dear repose for limbs with travel tired ;
> But then begins a journey in my head
> To work my mind, when body's work's expired.*

That Bacon sought the help of medicinal waters is proved by a letter which he wrote to Essex in 1594 :

> . . . as for appetite, the waters of Parnassus are not like the waters of the Spaw that give a stomach ; but rather they quench appetite and desires.

Essex had been urging the claims of Bacon for the office of solicitor-general then vacant. Burleigh opposed this, and was using his influence with the Queen on behalf of his son, Robert Cecil. The law was distasteful to Bacon as, he wrote to Essex in the same letter, " It drinketh too much time which I have devoted to better purposes ". His appetite had been quenched by " the waters of Parnassus ".

On 11th September, 1593, Bacon wrote to his mother mentioning his intention of making a journey to Bath. This letter is preserved among several volumes of correspondence exchanged between the Bacons, Essex and others, at Lambeth Palace. It is filed in Vol. III, folio 208, of the Lambeth manuscripts.

* See page 32.

VI

" A Lover's Complaint "

THIS curious poem was first printed at the end of the Sonnets in 1609. It is not written in sonnet form, but in seven line stanzas. Everything about it indicates an early composition, and we shall never know how or where the manuscript was preserved, or how it came into the hands of Thomas Thorpe, the publisher. As we shall see, the poem and the Sonnets are correlative, and presumably both were handed to Thorpe, probably by " Mr. W.H.", at the same time.

Although included in every complete edition of Shakespeare, *A Lover's Complaint* is *terra incognita* except to a very limited number of Shakespearean students. As in the case of the Sonnets, those who have attempted to judge the poem are at variance as to its merit and meaning. Some have questioned Shakespeare's authorship and most of the editors and commentators dismiss it with the fewest possible words without so much as a theory as to its meaning. The reference to it by the late Sir Sidney Lee is typical :

> Although its metre is that of *Lucrece,* it has no other affinity with Shakespeare's poetic style. Throughout the language is strained and the imagery far-fetched. Many awkward words appear for the first and only time, and their invention seems due to the author's imperfect command of the available poetic vocabulary.

My comment upon this is that Shakespeare used a great many awkward words both in the plays and poems. They were of his own coinage, and he added some 8,000 new words to our language mostly of Latin derivation. What Sir Sidney Lee overlooked is that there may be good grounds for the use of awkward words in the poem other than the alleged " imperfect command of the available poetic vocabulary ". It is unreasonable to doubt Shakespeare's authorship because it compares unfavourably with other writings bearing his name. A poet

must have a beginning, and although *Venus and Adonis* (1593)
was stated by its author to be " the first heir of my invention ",
it bears the stamp of former practical experience in the many
literary devices and poetical figures discussed in *The Arte of
English Poesie* (1589). That poem is far too perfect to be any
man's first-born. If the *Complaint* be a production of his
youth, it might very well account for some of the difficulties the
critics have experienced in accepting Shakespeare's authorship.

It is, however, my belief that the use of the unusual vocabulary
was necessitated by the nature of the poem which, as I shall
endeavour to show, deserves more attention than has been given
to it; for everything points to there being yet another variation
of Shakespeare's protean genius which has still to be explored.

We seem to come into contact with the allegorical and allusive
vocabulary of the writers of enigmatical poetry. This being so,
it would be unjust to compare the clear and straightforward
style of a narrative poem with an esoteric work teeming with
obscurities and veiling hidden meanings. By treating it as an
allegory, it is surprising with what ease the principal characters
and the setting of the poem can be determined.

The " Complaint " is made by a Shepherdess (the lover) who
laments her seduction by an effeminate-looking, passionate and
eloquent Youth. The scene is laid by the banks of a stream
in the neighbourhood of a conspicuous Hill. Several verses are
occupied with the description of a fiery Horse, and the Youth's
control of it.

It would, indeed, be astonishing if these familiar associations
of Poetry had come together by accident, and I now submit the
following key to the interpretation of the poem :

The Hill	Parnassus
The River	Hippocrene
The beautiful Youth	The spirit of Poetry
The Shepherdess	Reason or Philosophy (now charmed and seduced by Poetry)
The Horse	Pegasus.

Hippocrene was the stream sacred to the Muses which flowed
from Parnassus. The spring rose from the ground when struck
by the feet of Pegasus—the winged horse of Poetry.*

* See Ovid *Met*. V, 5.

The opening lines of the poem aroused my curiosity and suspicion as to the setting :

> From off a hill whose concave womb re-worded
> A plaintful story from a sistering vale,

for Parnassus was said by the poets to have two peaks, and the echoing cavity is the valley between them. The district of " the bi-cliff hill ", as Drayton called it, abounded in pleasant valleys suitable for meditation.

The shepherdess is seated by the stream lamenting in the same vein of passion as Shakespeare uses in Sonnet 29 (in which he says, " I all alone beweep my outcast state ") for " Oft did she heave her napkin to her eyne." She is described as " the carcase of a beauty spent and done ".

In the second verse it is said that :

> Time had not scythed all that youth begun,
> Nor youth all quit ; but spite of heaven's fell rage,
> Some beauty peep'd through lattice of sear'd age.

These lines are paralleled in Sonnet 3, where the same metaphor is employed :

> So thou through *windows* of thine age shalt see
> Despite of wrinkles this thy golden time.

The shepherdess begins her complaint :

> Though in me you behold
> The injury of many a blasting hour,
> Let it not tell your judgment I am old ;
> Not age, but sorrow, over me hath power.

In the Sonnets, Shakespeare frequently dwells upon the effects of Time upon his features, and in Nos. 62 and 63 takes comfort that he will " ever live young " in his verse. And so we find the shepherdess consoling herself with " not age . . . over me hath power ".

She is now ensnared in the wiles of Poetry (as represented by the seductive Youth) and her actions and description have clearly become those of the poet :

> Sometimes her levell'd eyes their carriage ride,
> As they did battery to the spheres intend ;
> Sometimes diverted their poor balls are tied
> To the orbed earth.

Here, then, is " the poet's eye in a fine frenzy rolling, doth glance from heaven to earth, from earth to heaven" (*Midsummer Night's Dream*, V, 1). Other indications which identify her as a poet are her " careless hand of pride ", " pale and pined cheek," and " loose negligence ". All this is in the fifth verse.

The Youth, who is the cause of the complaint, is no rustic swain. He is, indeed, the spirit of poetry and eloquence :

> His qualities were beauteous as his form,
> For maiden-tongued he was, and thereof *free* ;
> Yet, if men mov'd him, was he such a storm
> As oft 'twixt May and April is to see,
> When winds breathe sweet, unruly though they be,
> His rudeness so with his *authoriz'd* youth,
> Did livery falseness in a pride of truth.

Poets are " free " and " authorised " and may take liberty with time, place, fact and circumstance. As Bacon says, poets may make " unlawful matches and divorces of things ". Sidney, in his *Defence of Poesie* defends " that high flying liberty of conceit proper to the poet ".

As to the youth's management of his fiery Pegasus, we are told :

> Well could he ride, and often men would say,
> " That horse his mettle from his rider takes :
> Proud of subjection, noble by the sway,
> What rounds, what bounds, what course, what stop he
>   makes ! "
> And controversy hence a question takes,
> Whether the horse by him became his deed,
> Or he his manage by the well-doing steed.

> But quickly on his side the verdict went :
> His real habitude gave life and grace
> To appertainings and to ornament,
> Accomplish'd in himself, not in his case :
> All aids, themselves made fairer by their place,
> Came for additions ; yet their purpos'd trim
> Piec'd not his grace, but were all grac'd by him.

The horse, with his rounds, bounds and stops, and the Youth's management of him is explained by that astute French critic, Taine, in his *Histoire de la Littérature Anglaise* (1865). He saw Shakespeare as an unrestrained genius, passionate and " d'une nature d'ésprit extraordinaire ". He did not have

A Lover's Complaint in his mind. I doubt very much if he ever read it, yet he might be accurately explaining the first of the two verses I have just quoted :

> Like a too fiery and powerful horse, he bounds, he cannot run. He bridges in a couple of words an enormous interval; is at the two poles in an instant.
>
> *(Translation.)*

The second of the above two verses appears on the surface to be quite inexplicable. Unless one is provided with the key to the interpretation of the poem, it could be read through many times and still be meaningless. What were these " appertainings " and " ornament ", " aids " and " additions " which were " all graced by him " ?

If you turn to *The Arte of English Poesie*, one of the great classics of the Elizabethan age, and printed by Richard Field in 1589, you will find the third book, which occupies more than half of this anonymous work, deals with " Ornament Poeticall ". The author says :

> This ornament we speak of is given to it by figures and figurative speeches, which be the flowers, as it were, and colours that a Poet setteth upon his language and art,

and again :

> Ornament is but the good or, rather, beautiful habit of language or style, and figurative speeches wherewith we burnish our language.

Next follow two verses on the " ornament " or embellishments which the Youth had at his command. It is the equipment of the dramatist's art and craft. The early critic, Steevens, who had no idea of the inner meaning of the poem, noticed this and observed that, " in these lines Shakespeare has accidentally delineated his own character as a dramatist ". The truth is that there is nothing accidental in the manner in which these tricks and qualities of the dramatist's art are introduced :

> So on the tip of his subduing tongue
> All kinds of arguments and question deep,
> All replication prompt, and reason strong,
> For his advantage still did wake and sleep :
> To make the weeper laugh, the laugher weep,

He had the dialect and different skill,
Catching all passions in his craft of will :

That he did in the general bosom reign*
Of young, of old, and sexes both enchanted,
To dwell with him in thoughts, or to remain
In personal duty, following where he haunted, etc.

Those lines allude to the persuasive force of poetry, especially
dramatic poetry ; it being, as the unknown author of *The Arte
of English Poesie* says :

A manner of utterance decked and set out with all manner
of fresh colours and figures, which maketh that it sooner
inveigleth the judgment of man, and carrieth his opinion this
way and that, whithersoever the heart, by impression of the
ear, shall be most affectionately bent and directed.

And as for the enchanting of young and old, we find Sidney
in his *Defence of Poesie* confirming this by saying that the poet :

Cometh with a tale which holdeth children from play and
old men from the chimney corner.

In *Love's Labour's Lost*, there is this description of the young
philosopher-poet, Biron :

Biron they call him ; but a merrier man,
Within the limit of becoming mirth,
I never spent an hour's talk withal :
His eye begets occasion for his wit ;
For every object that the one doth catch,
The other turns to a mirth-moving jest,
Which his fair tongue—conceit's expositor—
Delivers in such apt and gracious words,
That *aged ears* play truant at his *tales*
And *younger* hearings are quite ravished ;
So sweet and voluble is his discourse.

Can we be surprised, therefore, that the shepherdess should
confess her " seduction " by the wiles and persuasive power of
poetry :

What with his art in youth, and youth in art,
Threw my affections in his charmed power.

In order to win their way into their hearers' minds, the
dramatists assumed a protean versatility, and metamorphosed

* " Thy bosom is endeared with all hearts." (*Sonnet* 31).

their souls in those of Kings, Princes, Courtiers, Soldiers, Divines, Physicians, Lawyers, Musicians, Artisans, or any other variation they chose to represent.

We find Shakespeare writing :

> I can add colours to the chameleon,
> Change shapes with Proteus for advantages ;

and Middleton proudly boasts :

> I will play the changeling,
> I'll change myself into a thousand shapes
> To court our brave spectators : I'll change my postures
> Into a thousand different variations
> To draw even ladies' eyes to follow mine ;
> I'll change my voice into a thousand tones
> To chain attention.

Such was the " art of craft " by which the shepherdess was enchanted, and caused her to exclaim :

> Ah me ! I fell ; and yet do question make
> What I should do again for such a sake.

The Youth boasts of the previous conquests he had made, and that though he " kept hearts in liveries " (i.e. in his service) he was himself " free " :

> And reigned commanding in his monarchy.

Here again the explanation is to be found in Sidney's *Defence of Poesie* : " Now herein of all Sciences is our Poet the *monarch.*"

We have many illustrations in the poem of the quick-changing and dramatic powers of the Youth. Lines 302-308 are to the point :

> In him a plenitude of subtle matter,
> Applied to cautels (i.e. *deceits*) all strange forms receives
> Of burning blushes, or of weeping water,
> Of swooning paleness ; and he takes and leaves,
> In either's aptness, as it best deceives,
> To blush at speeches rank, to weep at woes,
> Or to turn white, and swoon at tragic shows.

So this seductive art is a " plenitude of subtle matter ", which is full of deceits and takes all kinds of " strange forms ". Three classes of these are mentioned—blushes, tears and paleness, caused respectively by " speeches rank ", " woes," and " tragic shows ". These are part of the dramatist's equipment whose art it is to represent the emotions. This power of assuming all forms, shapes, colours and passions belongs to what our poet calls " invention ". There is a further subtle allusion to it in the last stanza :

> O, that infected (i.e. feigned) moisture of his eye !
> O, that false fire which in his cheeks so glow'd !
> O, that forced thunder from his heart did fly !
> O, that sad breath his spongy lungs bestow'd !
> O, all that borrow'd motion, seeming ow'd (i.e. his own) !

Having reviewed the main features of this strange poem, there remain several points of interest still to be discussed. The opening stanzas depict the shepherdess weeping by the river, tearing papers and breaking posied rings. These she throws into the stream. In the seventh verse we hear more about them :

> Of folded schedules had she many a one,
> Which she perus'd, sigh'd, tore and gave the flood ;
> Crack'd many a ring of posied gold and bone,
> Bidding them find their sepulchres in mud ;
> Found yet more letters sadly penn'd in blood,
> > With sleided silk, feat and affectedly,
> > Enswath'd and sealed to curious secrecy.

" Folded " means *enfolded* or *enigmatical,* and these writings and letters are treated in the same way as Prospero (a later personification of Shakespeare himself) intended to do with his " book ". From the thirty-first verse we learn that the " folded schedules " were " deep-brained sonnets ", and these had been dedicated to the Youth by former " lovers ". These sonnets had, in turn, been yielded up to the Shepherdess. They are said to have been " penned in blood "—an ingenious expression to conceal poetic impulse. It is the reproof of others for the exercising of his " sportive blood " which Shakespeare in Sonnet 121 takes so much to heart, and we find the Shepherdess harping upon the same string :

> Nor gives it satisfaction to our blood
> That we must curb it upon others' proof (i.e. *reproof*).

It alludes to the adverse criticism meted out to him in certain quarters, and Sonnets 70 and 72 inform us that he was held up to shame by his critics :

> For I am shamed by that which I bring forth.

In the Satires of Joseph Hall, printed in 1597, the author of *Venus and Adonis* was attacked under the name of *Labeo* for the licentious subject he had chosen, and for concealing his identity under another name.   Hall was a bigoted puritan and afterwards became Bishop of Norwich.   He begins the second book of his Satires with the line :

> For shame ! write better, Labeo, or write none,

and the last line of all is :

> For shame ! write cleanly, Labeo, or write none.

Antistius Labeo was a celebrated lawyer in the time of Augustus. He lost favour with the Emperor for opposing his views.   He is said to have enjoyed the company and conversation of learned men for six months of the year, and the rest was spent in writing and composing.   His works are either lost or are known under another name or names.   Bacon, in 1593, emphasized his objections in the House of Commons to the Lords interfering with the rights of the Commons on the issue of an increased subsidy for financing the secret service engaged on the discovery of alleged Popish plots.   His views were not well received at Court, and the Queen showed her annoyance at the utterances he had made.

The *Lover's Complaint* finds its best commentary in the Sonnets.   It would take up too much space to point out and discuss the many identities of thought, phrase and meaning, but we can scarcely ignore the nature of " Love " in them.

It is described as " eternal love " (S. 108) and " religious love " (S. 31).   Where can this " eternal love " be if not in immortal lines?   Does not " our ever-living poet " promise eternity in his sonnets?   He is confident his lines are " eternal numbers to out-live long date ".   In the *Complaint* the allusion to " eternal love " occurs in the thirty-fourth verse in reference to a former " lover " :

> Which late her noble suit in court did shun
> . . . and did thence remove
> To spend her living in eternal love.

Who is represented by this lover of poetry who withdrew from the Court to become a votarist in Apollo's temple? Still recording the story of this " nun ", the youth tells how, having been subdued to his will, she fled the " caged cloister " :

> Religious love put out religion's eye :
> Not to be tempted would she be immured,
> And now to tempt, all liberty procured.

The reason why this very obscure allusion to " religious love " is introduced is explained in *The Arte of English Poesie*. In Book I, Ch. 3, when telling of the origin of poets, the author says that they were " the first priests and ministers of the holy mysteries ", and established " ceremonies of religion ". They " lived chaste and in all holiness of life ". By continual study and meditation they came by divine instinct " to receive visions both waking and sleeping, which made them utter prophesies, and foretell things to come ". Note how Shakespeare in Sonnet 107 speaks of prophesy and " dreaming on things to come ".

It cannot be a mere coincidence that in Sonnet 31 " religious love " is also allied to the eye :

> How many a holy and obsequious tear
> Hath dear religious love *stolen* from mine eye !

And this brings us back to the key-sonnet (No. 20) :

> Which *steals* men's eyes and women's souls amazeth.

What " liberty " did this nun procure? Was it the liberty desired by Jaques in *As You Like It*?

> I must have liberty,
> Withal as large a charter as the wind
> To blow on whom I please. . . .
> Invest me in my motley, give me leave
> To speak my mind, and I will through and through
> Cleanse the foul body of the infected world
> If they will patiently receive my medicine.

Surely that is the voice of Shakespeare himself.

Poetry, and especially dramatic poetry, is the most licensed form of utterance. Poets, as I have mentioned, are authorized libertines in Time, Place and History.

Shakespeare's allegorical poems (and we must include the puzzling *Phoenix and Turtle* under this heading) were written in an age when writing in parable was not by any means rare. Bacon was master of the art of dissimulation, and, in his Preface to *The Wisdom of the Ancients* says of the ancient myths :

> It may pass for a further indication of a concealed and secret meaning that some of these fables are so absurd and idle in their narration as to show and proclaim an allegory even afar off.

On the surface *A Lover's Complaint* is so absurd and idle, being without apparent meaning or purpose, that it does " proclaim an allegory ", and the search for its inner meaning is certainly justified by the guide which Bacon gives to the presence of some such concealment.

Appendix I

The Date of Composition

ALTHOUGH first published in 1609, there is indisputable evidence that the Sonnets were written at intervals over a period of approximately ten years covering 1593-1603. We shall never know where the manuscripts remained during the interval of six years before publication, nor how they came into the hands of Thomas Thorpe; but it is generally accepted that he printed the Quarto from copies arranged into reasonably good grouping and sequence, though he failed to correct many obvious mistakes made by the scrivener.

Of the first 136 sonnets of the 154 collected, the evidence of parallels in thought, style and vocabulary is illuminating as to the period of composition. Patient and lengthy study and application show that the earlier writings of Shakespeare are by far the most productive. Plays accepted as having been written after 1603 scarcely yield any parallelisms. Thus, while the poem " Venus and Adonis " gives no less than 64, only two can be traced in " The Tempest " and those are confined to thought and not expression. The result of this enquiry shows these parallelisms noted :

Venus and Adonis	1592/3	64
Lucrece	1593/4	60
M.N. Dream	1593/5	45
L.L. Lost	1590/1	49
Romeo and Juliet	1591/4	48
Richard II	1595	26
Richard III	1593	24

There is a gradual decline in the number applicable to plays written after 1595. " Hamlet " (1602-04) gives 15 after which few of the plays even show double figures.

The character of the parallelisms is important, and one must ignore those which are conventional ideas and expressions.

Unfortunately the Sonnets contain few allusions to contemporary events. There is, however, one which undoubtedly alludes to the death of Queen Elizabeth in 1603, and the civil

E

war which it was feared might follow through which the arts would perish, since she had not named her successor. The reference to this occurs in Sonnet 107 :

> Not mine own fears, nor the prophetic soul
> Of the wide world dreaming on things to come
> Can yet the lease of my true love control,
> Supposed as forfeit to a confin'd doom.
> The mortal moon hath her eclipse endur'd*
> And the sad augurs mock their own presage ;
> Incertainties now *crown* themselves assur'd
> And *peace* proclaims olives of endless age.

One has only to compare these lines with the opening paragraph of the Dedication of the Authorized Version of the Bible to King James as to the fears which were generally held as to what might follow, and how the crowning of King James brought the assurance of peace and tranquillity :

> For whereas it was the expectation of many who wished not well unto our Sion that upon the setting of that bright occidental star, Queen Elizabeth of most happy memory, some thick and palpable clouds of darkness would so have over-shadowed this land that men should have been in doubt which way they were to walk, and that it should hardly be known who was to direct the unsettled State ; the appearance of your Majesty, as of the sun in his strength, instantly dispelled those supposed and surmised mists, and gave unto all . . . peace and tranquillity.

Bacon, in his brief memoir of the Queen, wrote :

> It had been generally dispersed abroad that after Queen Elizabeth's death, there must follow in England nothing but confusions, interreigns and perturbations of estate; likely far to exceed the ancient calamities of the civil wars between the houses of Lancaster and York.

Elizabeth herself prognosticated that her death would be followed by the overthrow of the Protestant religion and the ruin of the realm.

That " the mortal moon " refers to the Queen is confirmed by other poets of that time. Cynthia (the moon) was a favourite appellation for her, and she so figures in Spenser, Barnfield, Raleigh and others.

There is no evidence that any of the Sonnets were written after 1603.

---

* Writing of another Queen Elizabeth, Bacon says in his *History of Henry VII,* " she had endured a strange eclipse ".

Appendix II

Henry Wriothesley, Earl of Southampton
1573-1624

Dr. A. L. Rowse, F.B.A., M.A., D.Litt., is a recognised authority on English History, particularly of the Elizabethan period.

Early in 1964 he published his *William Shakespeare* which had a very mixed reception from the reviewers and Shakespeareans generally. The arrogance with which he presented his " discoveries " as to the meaning of the Sonnets, and his contempt for those who held other opinions, were particularly irritating. " Discoveries " for which he claimed credit were not always new. One was that " the rival poet " of Sonnets 76-86 was Marlowe who died in 1593—the year when the name of Shakespeare is first used in connection with poetry, and four years before any of the Plays were printed. Marlowe was first named as the " rival " by Gerald Massey in *The Secret Drama of Shakespeare's Sonnets* in 1888, but apart from Parke Godwin in his *New Study of the Sonnets* in 1900, the theory has received little support.

Dr. Rowse will have none other than the Earl of Southampton for the " friend ". He is intolerant of any other view. The image on which Shakespeare lavishes his affection and admiration has " a woman's face " and " a woman's gentle heart " (Sonnet 20). One would have thought that, as a historian, Dr. Rowse would have looked into the nature and character of the Earl. What emerges is a man of martial ardour and violent temperament. He proved his gallantry on the Cadiz and Azores expeditions of 1595-96, and in 1599 went with Essex as his Master of Horse on the ill-fated Irish expedition. In the following year he joined Essex in his disastrous rebellion with the idea of deposing the elderly Queen. For his part in it he was imprisoned in the Tower until released by King James in 1603.

Even at the age of 51, he led a body of English volunteers to help the Dutch against the Spaniards.

Was Dr. Rowse acquainted with these facts and yet ignored them because they did not conform with his preconceived theory?

SHAKE-SPEARES

SONNETS.

Neuer before Imprinted.

AT LONDON
By *G. Eld* for *T. T.* and are
to be solde by *Iohn Wright*, dwelling
at Chrift Church gate.
1609.

TO . THE . ONLIE . BEGETTER . OF .
THESE . INSVING . SONNETS .
Mr. W. H. ALL . HAPPINESSE .
AND . THAT . ETERNITIE .
PROMISED .

BY .

OVR . EVER-LIVING . POET .

WISHETH .

THE . WELL-WISHING .
ADVENTVRER . IN .
SETTING .
FORTH .

T. T.

SHAKE-SPEARES,
SONNETS.

FRom faireſt creatures we deſire increaſe,
　　That thereby beauties *Roſe* might neuer die,
But as the riper ſhould by time deceaſe,
His tender heire might beare his memory:
But thou contracted to thine owne bright eyes,
Feed'ſt thy lights flame with ſelfe ſubſtantiall fewell,
Making a famine where aboundance lies,
Thy ſelfe thy foe, to thy ſweet ſelfe too cruell:
Thou that art now the worlds freſh ornament,
And only herauld to the gaudy ſpring,
Within thine owne bud burieſt thy content,
And tender chorle makſt waſt in niggarding:
　　Pitty the world, or elſe this glutton be,
　　To eate the worlds due, by the graue and thee.

2

VVHen fortie Winters ſhall beſeige thy brow,
　　And digge deep trenches in thy beauties field,
Thy youthes proud liuery ſo gaz'd on now,
Wil be a totter'd weed of ſmal worth held:
Then being askt, where all thy beautie lies,
Where all the treaſure of thy luſty daies;
To ſay within thine owne deepe ſunken eyes,
Were an all-eating ſhame, and thriftleſſe praiſe.
How much more praiſe deſeru'd thy beauties vſe,
If thou couldſt anſwere this faire child of mine
Shall ſum my count, and make my old excuſe
Proouing his beautie by ſucceſſion thine.

B

This

This were to be new made when thou art ould,
And see thy blood warme when thou feel'ſt it could.

3

Looke in thy glaſſe and tell the face thou veweſt,
Now is the time that face ſhould forme an other,
Whoſe freſh repaire if now thou not reneweſt,
Thou doo'ſt beguile the world, vnbleſſe ſome mother.
For where is ſhe ſo faire whoſe vn-eard wombe
Diſdaines the tillage of thy husbandry?
Or who is he ſo fond will be the tombe,
Of his ſelfe loue to ſtop poſterity?
Thou art thy mothers glaſſe and ſhe in thee
Calls backe the louely Aprill of her prime,
So thou through windowes of thine age ſhalt ſee,
Diſpight of wrinkles this thy goulden time.
　But if thou liue remembred not to be,
　Die ſingle and thine Image dies with thee.

4

Vnthrifty louelineſſe why doſt thou ſpend,
Vpon thy ſelfe thy beauties legacy?
Natures bequeſt giues nothing but doth lend,
And being franck ſhe lends to thoſe are free:
Then beautious nigard why dooſt thou abuſe,
The bountious largeſſe giuen thee to giue?
Profitles vſerer why dooſt thou vſe
So great a ſumme of ſummes yet can'ſt not liue?
For hauing traffike with thy ſelfe alone,
Thou of thy ſelfe thy ſweet ſelfe doſt deceaue,
Then how when nature calls thee to be gone,
What acceptable _Audit_ can'ſt thou leaue?
　Thy vnuſ'd beauty muſt be tomb'd with thee,
　Which vſed liues th'executor to be.

5

Thoſe howers that with gentle worke did frame,
The louely gaze where euery eye doth dwell
Will play the tirants to the very ſame,

And

And that vnfaire which fairely doth excell:
For euer resting time leads Summer on,
To hidious winter and consounds him there,
Sap checkt with frost and lustie leau's quite gon.
Beauty ore-snow'd and barenes euery where,
Then were not summers distillation left
A liquid prisoner pent in walls of glasse,
Beauties effect with beauty were bereft,
Nor it nor noe remembrance what it was.
    But flowers distil'd though they with winter meete,
    Leese but their show, their substance still liues sweet.

6

THen let not winters wragged hand deface,
  In thee thy summer ere thou be distil'd:
Make sweet some viall; treasure thou some place,
With beautits treasure ere it be selfe kil'd:
That vse is not forbidden vsery,
Which happies those that pay the willing lone;
That's for thy selfe to breed an other thee,
Or ten times happier be it ten for one,
Ten times thy selfe were happier then thou art,
If ten of thine ten times refigur d thee,
Then what could death doe if thou should'st depart,
Leauing thee liuing in posterity?
    Be not selfe-wild for thou art much too faire,
    To be deaths conquest and make wormes thine heire.

7

LOe in the Orient when the gracious light,
  Lifts vp his burning head, each vnder eye
Doth homage to his new appearing sight,
Seruing with lookes his sacred maiesty,
And hauing climb'd the steepe vp heauenly hill,
Resembling strong youth in his middle age,
Yet mortall lookes adore his beauty still,
Attending on his goulden pilgrimage:
But when from high-most pich with wery car,

Like feeble age he reeleth from the day,
The eyes(fore dutious)now conuerted are
From his low tract and looke an other way:
   So thou,thy felfe out-going in thy noon:
   Vnlok'd on dieft vnleſſe thou get a fonne.

8

MVſick to heare,why hear'ſt thou muſick ſadly,
Sweets with ſweets warre not ,ioy delights in ioy:
Why lou'ſt thou that which thou receauſt not gladly,
Or elſe receau'ſt with pleaſure thine annoy ?
If the true concord of well tuned ſounds,
By vnions married do offend thine eare,
They do but ſweetly chide thee, who confounds
In ſingleneſſe the parts that thou ſhould'ſt beare:
Marke how one ſtring ſweet husband to an other,
Strike each in each by mutuall ordering;
Reſembling ſier,and child, and happy mother,
Who all in one,one pleaſing note do ſing:
   Whoſe ſpeechleſſe ſong being many,ſeeming one,
   Sings this to thee thou ſingle wilt proue none.

9.

IS it for feare to wet a widdowes eye,
That thou conſum'ſt thy ſelfe in ſingle life?
Ah;if thou iſſuleſſe ſhalt hap to die,
The world will waile thee like a makeleſſe wife,
The world wilbe thy widdow and ſtill weepe,
That thou no forme of thee haſt left behind,
When euery priuat widdow well may keepe,
By childrens eyes,her husbands ſhape in minde:
Looke what an vnthrift in the world doth ſpend
Shifts but his place,for ſtill the world inioyes it
But beauties waſte, hath in the world an end,
And kept vnvſde the vſer ſo deſtroyes it:
   No loue toward others in that boſome ſits
   That on himſelfe ſuch murdrous ſhame commits.

10

FOr shame deny that thou bear'st loue to any
Who for thy selfe art so vnprouident
Graunt if thou wilt,thou art belou'd of many,
But that thou none lou'st is most euident:
For thou art so possest with murdrous hate,
That gainst thy selfe thou stickst not to conspire,
Seeking that beautious roofe to ruinate
Which to repaire should be thy chiefe desire :
O change thy thought,that I may change my minde,
Shall hate be fairer log'd then gentle loue?
Be as thy presence is gracious and kind,
Or to thy selfe at least kind harted proue,
 Make thee an other selfe for loue of me,
 That beauty still may liue in thine or thee.

11

AS fast as thou shalt wane so fast thou grow'st,
In one of thine,from that which thou departest,
And that fresh bloud which yongly thou bestow'st,
Thou maist call thine,when thou from youth conuertest,
Herein liues wisdome,beauty,and increase,
Without this follie,age,and could decay,
If all were minded so,the times should cease,
And threescoore yeare would make the world away:
Let those whom nature hath not made for store,
Harsh,featurelesse,and rude , barrenly perrish,
Looke whom she best indow'd,she gaue the more;
Which bountious guift thou shouldst in bounty cherrish,
 She caru'd thee for her seale,and ment therby,
 Thou shouldst print more,not let that coppy die.

12

VVHen I doe count the clock that tels the time,
 And see the braue day sunck in hidious night,
When I behold the violet past prime,
And sable curls or siluer'd ore with white :
When lofty trees I see barren of leaues,
Which erst from heat did canopie the herd

And

And Sommers greene all girded vp in ſheaues
Borne on the beare with white and briſtly beard:
Then of thy beauty do I queſtion make
That thou among the waſtes of time muſt goe,
Since ſweets and beauties do them-ſelues forſake,
  And die as faſt as they ſee others grow,
    And nothing gainſt Times ſieth can make defence
    Saue breed to braue him,when he takes thee hence.

13

O That you were your ſelfe,but loue you are
  No longer yours,then you your ſelfe here liue,
Againſt this cumming end you ſhould prepare,
And your ſweet ſemblance to ſome other giue.
So ſhould that beauty which you hold in leaſe
Find no determination,then you were
You ſelfe again after your ſelfes deceaſe,
When your ſweet iſſue your ſweet forme ſhould beare.
Who lets ſo faire a houſe fall to decay,
Which husbandry in honour might vphold,
Againſt the ſtormy guſts of winters day
And barren rage of deaths eternall cold?
  O none but vnthrifts,deare my loue you know,
  You had a Father,let your Son ſay ſo.

14

NOt fron the ſtars do I my iudgement plucke,
  And yet me thinkes I haue Aſtronomy,
But not to tell of good,or euil lucke,
Of plagues,of dearths,or ſeaſons quallity,
Nor can I fortune to breeſe mynuits tell;
Pointing to each his thunder, raine and winde,
Or ſay with Princes if it ſhal go wel
By oft predict that I in heauen finde,
But from thine eies my knowledge I deriue,
And conſtant ſtars in them I read ſuch art
As truth and beautie ſhal together thriue
If from thy ſelfe,to ſtore thou wouldſt conuert:

Or else ofthee this I prognosticate,
  Thy end is Truthes and Beauties doome and date.

15

WHen I confider euery thing that growes
  Holds in perfection but a little moment.
That this huge ftage prefenteth nought but fhowes
Whereon the Stars in fecret influence comment.
When I perceiue that men as plants increafe,
Cheared and checkt euen by the felfe-fame skie:
Vaunt in their youthfull fap,at height decreafe,
And were their braue ftate out of memory.
Then the conceit of this inconftant ftay,
Sets you moft rich in youth before my fight,
Where waftfull time debateth with decay
To change your day of youth to fullied night,
    And all in war with Time for loue of you
    As he takes from you,I ingraft you new.

16

BVt wherefore do not you a mightier waie
  Make warre vppon this bloudie tirant time?
And fortifie your felfe in your decay
With meanes more bleffed then my barren rime?
Now ftand you on the top of happie houres,
And many maiden gardens yet vnfet,
With vertuous wifh would beare your liuing flowers,
Much liker then your painted counterfeit:
So fhould the lines of life that life repaire
Which this (Times penfel or my pupill pen)
Neither in inward worth nor outward faire
Can make you liue your felfe in eies of men,
    To giue away your felfe,keeps your felfe ftill,
    And you muft liue drawne by your owne fweet skill,

17

VVHo will beleeue my verfe in time to come
  If it were fild with your moft high deferts?

                 Though

Though yet heauen knowes it is but as a tombe
Which hides your life , and shewes not halfe your parts:
If I could write the beauty of your eyes,
And in fresh numbers number all your graces,
The age to come would say this Poet lies,
Such heauenly touches nere toucht earthly faces.
So should my papers (yellowed with their age)
Be scorn'd,like old men of lesse truth then tongue,
And your true rights be termd a Poets rage,
And stretched miter of an Antique song.
　　But were some childe of yours aliue that time.
　　You should liue twise in it,and in my rime.

18.

SHall I compare thee to a Summers day?
　　Thou art more louely and more temperate:
Rough windes do shake the darling buds of Maie,
And Sommers lease hath all too short a date:
Sometime too hot the eye of heauen shines,
And often is his gold complexion dimm'd,
And euery faire from faire some-time declines,
By chance,or natures changing course vntrim'd:
But thy eternall Sommer shall not fade,
Nor loose possession of that faire thou ow'st,
Nor shall death brag thou wandr'st in his shade,
When in eternall lines to time thou grow'st,
　　So long as men can breath or eyes can see,
　　So long liues this,and this giues life to thee,

19

DEuouring time blunt thou the Lyons pawes,
　　And make the earth deuoure her owne sweet brood,
Plucke the keene teeth from the fierce Tygers yawes,
And burne the long liu'd Phænix in her blood,
Make glad and sorry seasons as thou fleet'st,
And do what ere thou wilt swift-footed time
To the wide world and all her fading sweets:
But I forbid thee one most hainous crime,

O

O carue not with thy howers my loues faire brow,
Nor draw noe lines there with thine antique pen,
Him in thy courſe vntainted doe allow,
For beauties patterne to ſucceding men.
  Yet doe thy worſt ould Time diſpight thy wrong,
  My loue ſhall in my verſe euer liue young.

20

A Womans face with natures owne hand painted,
  Haſte thou the Maſter Miſtris of my paſſion,
A womans gentle hart but not acquainted
With ſhifting change as is falſe womens faſhion,
An eye more bright then theirs, leſſe falſe in rowling:
Gilding the obiect where-vpon it gazeth,
A man in hew all *Hews* in his controwling,
Which ſteales mens eyes and womens ſoules amaſeth.
And for a woman wert thou firſt created,
Till nature as ſhe wrought thee fell a dotinge,
And by addition me of thee defeated,
By adding one thing to my purpoſe nothing.
  But ſince ſhe prickt thee out for womens pleaſure,
  Mine be thy loue and thy loues vſe their treaſure.

21

SO is it not with me as with that Muſe,
  Stird by a painted beauty to his verſe,
Who heauen it ſelfe for ornament doth vſe,
And euery faire with his faire doth reherſe,
Making a coopelment of proud compare
With Sunne and Moone, with earth and ſeas rich gems:
With Aprills firſt borne flowers and all things rare,
That heauens ayre in this huge rondure hems,
O let me true in loue but truly write,
And then beleeue me, my loue is as faire,
As any mothers childe, though not ſo bright
As thoſe gould candells fixt in heauens ayer:
  Let them ſay more that like of heare-ſay well,
  I will not prayſe that purpoſe not to ſell.

C   22

F

22

MY glasse shall not perswade me I am ould,
So long as youth and thou are of one date,
But when in thee times forrwes I behould,
Then look I death my daies should expiate.
For all that beauty that doth couer thee,
Is but the seemely rayment of my heart,
Which in thy brest doth liue,as thine in me,
How can I then be elder then thou art?
O therefore loue be of thy selfe so wary,
As I not for my selfe,but for thee will,
Bearing thy heart which I will keepe so chary
As tender nurse her babe from faring ill,
　　Presume not on thy heart when mine is slaine,
　　Thou gau'st me thine not to giue backe againe.

23

AS an vnperfect actor on the stage,
Who with his feare is put besides his part,
Or some fierce thing repleat with too much rage,
Whose strengths abondance weakens his owne heart;
So I for feare of trust,forget to say,
The perfect ceremony of loues right,
And in mine owne loues strength seeme to decay,
Ore-charg'd with burthen of mine owne loues might:
O let my books be then the eloquence,
And domb presagers of my speaking brest,
Who pleade for loue,and look for-recompence,
More then that tonge that more hath more exprest.
　　O learne to read what silent loue hath writ,
　　To heare wit eies belongs to loues fine wiht.

24

MIne eye hath play'd the painter and hath steeld,
Thy beauties forme in table of my heart,
My body is the frame wherein ti's held,
And perspectiue it is best Painters art.
For through the Painter must you see his skill,

To finde where your true Image pictur'd lies,
Which in my bosomes shop is hanging stil,
That hath his windowes glazed with thine eyes:
Now see what good-turnes eyes for-eies haue done,
Mine eyes haue drawne thy shape, and thine for me
Are windowes to my brest, where-through the Sun
Delights to peepe, to gaze therein on thee
    Yet eyes this cunning want to grace their art
    They draw but what they see, know not the hart.

25

LEt those who are in fauor with their stars,
  Of publike honour and proud titles bost,
Whilst I whome fortune of such tryumph bars
Vnlookt for ioy in that I honour most;
Great Princes fauorites their faire leaues spread,
But as the Marygold at the suns eye,
And in them-selues their pride lies buried,
For at a frowne they in their glory die.
The painefull warrier famosed for worth,
After a thousand victories once foild,
Is from the booke of honour rased quite,
And all the rest forgot for which he toild:
    Then happy I that loue and am beloued
    Where I may not remoue, nor be remoued.

26

LOrd of my loue, to whome in vassalage
  Thy merrit hath my dutie strongly knit;
To thee I send this written ambassage
To witnesse duty, not to shew my wit.
Duty so great, which wit so poore as mine
May make seeme bare, in wanting words to shew it;
But that I hope some good conceipt of thine
In thy soules thought (all naked) will bestow it:
Til whatsoeuer star that guides my mouing,
Points on me gratiously with faire aspect,
And puts apparrell on my tottered louing,

To ſhow me worthy of their ſweet reſpect,
 Then may I dare to boaſt how I doe loue thee,
 Til then,not ſhow my head where thou maiſt proue me

27

WEary with toyle,I haſt me to my bed,
 The deare repoſe for lims with trauaill tired,
But then begins a iourny in my head
To worke my mind,when boddies work's expired.
For then my thoughts(from far where I abide)
Intend a zelous pilgrimage to thee;
And keepe my drooping eye-lids open wide,
Looking on darknes which the blind doe ſee.
Saue that my ſoules imaginary ſight
Preſents their ſhaddoe to my ſightles view,
Which like a iewell(hunge in gaſtly night)
Makes blacke night beautious,and her old face new.
 Loe thus by day my lims,by night my mind,
 For thee,and for my ſelfe,noe quiet finde.

28

HOw can I then returne in happy plight
 That am debard the benifit of reſt?
When daies oppreſſion is not eazd by night,
But day by night and night by day opreſt.
And each(though enimes to ethers raigne)
Doe in conſent ſhake hands to torture me,
The one by toyle,the other to complaine
How far I toyle,ſtill farther off from thee.
I tell the Day to pleaſe him thou art bright,
And do'ſt him grace when clouds doe blot the heauen:
So flatter I the ſwart complexiond night,
When ſparkling ſtars twire not thou guil'ſt th' eauen.
 But day doth daily draw my ſorrowes longer,(ſtronger
 And night doth nightly make greefes length ſeeme

29

VVHen in diſgrace with Fortune and mens eyes,
 I all alone beweepe my out-caſt ſtate,

And

And trouble deafe heauen with my bootlesse cries,
And looke vpon my selfe and curse my sate.
Wishing me like to one more rich in hope,
Featur'd like him, like him with friends possest,
Desiring this mans art, and that mans skope,
With what I most inioy contented least,
Yet in these thoughts my selfe almost despising,
Haplye I thinke on thee, and then my state,
(Like to the Larke at breake of daye arising)
From sullen earth sings himns at Heauens gate,
    For thy sweet loue remembred such welth brings,
    That then I skorne to change my state with Kings.

30

VVHen to the Sessions of sweet silent thought,
    I sommon vp remembrance of things past,
I sigh the lacke of many a thing I sought,
And with old woes new waile my deare times waste:
Then can I drowne an eye (vn-vs'd to flow)
For precious friends hid in deaths dateles night,
And weepe a fresh loues long since canceld woe,
And mone th'expence of many a vannisht sight.
Then can I greeue at greeuances fore-gon,
And heauily from woe to woe tell ore
The sad account of fore-bemoned mone,
Which I new pay, as if not payd before.
    But if the while I thinke on thee (deare friend)
    All losses are restord, and sorrowes end.

31

Thy bosome is indeared with all hearts,
    Which I by lacking haue supposed dead,
And there raignes Loue and all Loues louing parts,
And all those friends which I thought buried.
How many a holy and obsequious teare
Hath deare religious loue stolne from mine eye,
As interest of the dead, which now appeare,
But things remou'd that hidden in there lie.

Thou art the graue where buried loue doth liue,
Hung with the tropheis of my louers gon,
Who all their parts of me to thee did giue,
That due of many, now is thine alone.
    Their images I lou'd, I view in thee,
    And thou(all they)haft all the all of me.

32

IF thou furuiue my well contented daie,
    When that churle death my bones with duft fhall couer
And fhalt by fortune once more re-furuay:
Thefe poore rude lines of thy deceafed Louer:
Compare them with the bett'ring of the time,
And though they be out-ftript by euery pen,
Referue them for my loue, not for their rime,
Exceeded by the hight of happier men.
Oh then voutfafe me but this louing thought,
Had my friends Mufe growne with this growing age,
A dearer birth then this his loue had brought
To march in ranckes of better equipage:
    But fince he died and Poets better proue,
    Theirs for their ftile ile read, his for his loue.

33

FVll many a glorious morning haue I feene,
    Flatter the mountaine tops with foueraine eie,
Kiffing with golden face the meddowes greene;
Guilding pale ftreames with heauenly alcumy:
Anon permit the bafeft cloudes to ride,
With ougly rack on his celeftiall face,
And from the for-lorne world his vifage hide
Stealing vnfeene to weft with this difgrace:
Euen fo my Sunne one early morne did fhine,
With all triumphant fplendor on my brow,
But out alack, he was but one houre mine,
The region cloude hath mask'd him from me now.
    Yet him for this, my loue no whit difdaineth,
    Suns of the world may ftaine, whē heauens fun ftainteh.

34

34

VVHy didſt thou promiſe ſuch a beautious day,
　And make me trauaile forth without my cloake,
To let baſe cloudes ore-take me in my way,
Hiding thy brau'ry in their rotten ſmoke.
Tis not enough that through the cloude thou breake,
To dry the raine on my ſtorme-beaten face,
For no man well of ſuch a ſalue can ſpeake,
That heales the wound, and cures not the diſgrace:
Nor can thy ſhame giue phiſicke to my griefe,
Though thou repent , yet I haue ſtill the loſſe,
Th' offenders ſorrow lends but weake relieſe
To him that beares the ſtrong offenſes loſſe.
　Ah but thoſe teares are pearle which thy loue ſheeds,
　And they are ritch, and ranſome all ill deeds.

35

NO more bee greeu'd at that which thou haſt done,
　Roſes haue thornes, and ſiluer fountaines mud,
Cloudes and eclipſes ſtaine both Moone and Sunne,
And loathſome canker liues in ſweeteſt bud.
All men make faults, and euen I in this,
Authorizing thy treſpas with compare,
My ſelfe corrupting ſaluing thy amiſſe,
Excuſing their ſins more then their ſins are;
For to thy ſenſuall fault I bring in ſence,
Thy aduerſe party is thy Aduocate,
And gainſt my ſelfe a lawfull plea commence,
Such ciuill war is in my loue and hate,
　That I an acceſſary needs muſt be,
　To that ſweet theefe which ſourely robs from me,

36

LEt me confeſſe that we two muſt be twaine,
　Although our vndeuided loues are one:
So ſhall thoſe blots that do with me remaine,
Without thy helpe, by me be borne alone.
In our two loues there is but one reſpect,

Though

Though in our liues a seperable spight,
Which though it alter not loues sole effect,
Yet doth it steale sweet houres from loues delight,
I may not euer-more acknowledge thee,
Least my bewailed guilt should do thee shame,
Nor thou with publike kindnesse honour me,
Vnlesse thou take that honour from thy name:
   But doe not so, I loue thee in such sort,
   As thou being mine, mine is thy good report.

37

AS a decrepit father takes delight,
  To see his actiue childe do deeds of youth,
So I, made lame by Fortunes dearest spight
Take all my comfort of thy worth and truth.
For whether beauty, birth, or wealth, or wit,
Or any of these all, or all, or more
Intitled in their parts, do crowned sit,
I make my loue ingrafted to this store:
So then I am not lame, poore, nor dispis'd,
Whilst that this shadow doth such substance giue,
That I in thy abundance am suffic'd,
And by a part of all thy glory liue:
   Looke what is best, that best I wish in thee,
   This wish I haue, then ten times happy me.

38

HOw can my Muse want subiect to inuent
  While thou dost breath that poor'st into my verse,
Thine owne sweet argument, to excellent,
For euery vulgar paper to rehearse:
Oh giue thy selfe the thankes if ought in me,
Worthy perusal stand against thy sight,
For who's so dumbe that cannot write to thee,
When thou thy selfe dost giue inuention light?
Be thou the tenth Muse, ten times more in worth
Then those old nine which rimers inuocate,
And he that calls on thee, let him bring forth

                                  Eternall

Eternal numbers to out-liue long date.
  If my flight Muse doe pleafe thefe curious daies,
  The paine be mine, but thine fhal be the praife.

39

OH how thy worth with manners may I finge,
    When thou art all the better part of me?
What can mine owne praife to mine owne felfe bring;
And what is't but mine owne when I praife thee,
Euen for this, let vs deuided liue,
And our deare loue loofe name of fingle one,
That by this feperation I may giue:
That due to thee which thou deferu'ft alone:
Oh abfence what a torment wou!dft thou proue,
Were it not thy foure leifure gaue fweet leaue,
To entertaine the time with thoughts of loue,
VVhich time and thoughts fo fweetly doft deceiue.
  And that thou teacheft how to make one twaine,
  By praifing him here who doth hence remaine.

40

TAke all my loues, my loue, yea take them all,
    What haft thou then more then thou hadft before?
No loue, my loue, that thou maift true loue call,
All mine was thine, before thou hadft this more:
Then if for my loue, thou my loue receiueft,
I cannot blame thee, for my loue thou vfeft,
But yet be blam'd, if thou this felfe deceaueft
By wilfull tafte of what thy felfe refufeft.
I doe forgiue thy robb'rie gentle theefe
Although thou fteale thee all my pouerty:
And yet loue knowes it is a greater griefe
To beare loues wrong, then hates knowne iniury.
  Lafciuious grace in whom all il wel fhowes,
  Kill me with fpights yet we muft not be foes.

41

THofe pretty wrongs that liberty commits,
    When I am fome-time abfent from thy heart,

D   Thy

Thy beautie, and thy yeares full well befits,
For still temptacion followes where thou art.
Gentle thou art, and therefore to be wonne,
Beautious thou art, therefore to be aſſailed.
And when a woman woes, what womans ſonne,
Will ſourely leaue her till he haue preuailed.
Aye me, but yet thou mighſt my ſeate forbeare,
And chide thy beauty, and thy ſtraying youth,
Who lead thee in their ryot euen there
Where thou art forſt to breake a two-fold truth:
 Hers by thy beauty tempting her to thee,
 Thine by thy beautie beeing falſe to me.

42

THat thou haſt her it is not all my griefe,
 And yet it may be ſaid I lou'd her deerely,
That ſhe hath thee is of my wayling cheefe,
A loſſe in loue that touches me more neerely.
Louing offendors thus I will excuſe yee,
Thou dooſt loue her, becauſe thou knowſt I loue her,
And for my ſake euen ſo doth ſhe abuſe me,
Suffring my friend for my ſake to approoue her,
If I looſe thee, my loſſe is my loues gaine,
And looſing her, my friend hath found that loſſe,
Both finde each other, and I looſe both twaine,
And both for my ſake lay on me this croſſe,
 But here's the ioy, my friend and I are one,
 Sweete flattery, then ſhe loues but me alone.

43

WHen moſt I winke then doe mine eyes beſt ſee,
 For all the day they view things vnreſpected,
But when I ſleepe, in dreames they looke on thee,
And darkely bright, are bright in darke directed.
Then thou whoſe ſhaddow ſhaddowes doth make bright,
How would thy ſhadowes forme, forme happy ſhow,
To the cleere day with thy much cleerer light,
When to vn-ſeeing eyes thy ſhade ſhines ſo?

        How

How would (I say)mine eyes be bleſſed made,
By looking on thee in the liuing day?
When in dead night their faire imperfect ſhade,
Through heauy ſleepe on ſightleſſe eyes doth ſtay?
   All dayes are nights to ſee till I ſee thee,
   And nights bright daies when dreams do ſhew thee me,

44

IF the dull ſubſtance of my fleſh were thought,
Iniurious diſtance ſhould not ſtop my way,
For then diſpight of ſpace I would be brought,
From limits ſarre remote, where thou dooſt ſtay,
No matter then although my foote did ſtand
Vpon the fartheſt earth remoou'd from thee,
For nimble thought can iumpe both ſea and land,
As ſoone as thinke the place where he would be.
But ah, thought kills me that I am not thought
To leape large lengths of miles when thou art gone,
But that ſo much of earth and water wrought,
I muſt attend, times leaſure with my mone.
   Receiuing naughts by elements ſo ſloe,
   But heauie teares, badges of eithers woe,

45

THe other two, ſlight ayre, and purging fire,
Are both with thee, where euer I abide,
The firſt my thought, the other my deſire,
Theſe preſent abſent with ſwift motion ſlide.
For when theſe quicker Elements are gone
In tender Embaſſie of loue to thee,
My life being made of foure, with two alone,
Sinkes downe to death, oppreſt with melancholie,
Vntill liues compoſition be recured,
By thoſe ſwift meſſengers return'd from thee,
Who euen but now come back againe aſſured,
Of their faire health, recounting it to me.
   This told, I ioy, but then no longer glad,
   I ſend them back againe and ſtraight grow ſad,

Mine

46

Mine eye and heart are at a mortall warre,
How to deuide the conquest of thy sight,
Mine eye,my heart their pictures sight would barre,
My heart,mine eye the freeedome of that right,
My heart doth plead that thou in him doost lye,
(A closet neuer pearst with christall eyes)
But the defendant doth that plea deny,
And sayes in him their faire appearance lyes.
To side this title is impannelled
A quest of thoughts,all tennants to the heart,
And by their verdict is determined
The cleere eyes moyitie,and he deare hearts part.
 As thus,mine eyes due is their outward part,
 And my hearts right,their inward loue of heart.

47

Betwixt mine eye and heart a league is tooke,
And each doth good turnes now vnto the other,
When that mine eye is famisht for a looke,
Or heart in loue with sighes himselfe doth smother;
With my loues picture then my eye doth feast,
And to the painted banquet bids my heart:
An other time mine eye is my hearts guest,
And in his thoughts of loue doth share a part.
So either by thy picture or my loue,
Thy selfe away,are present still with me,
For thou nor farther then my thoughts canst moue,
And I am still with them,and they with thee.
 Or if they sleepe,thy picture in my sight
 Awakes my heart,to hearts and eyes delight.

48

How carefull was I when I tooke my way,
Each trifle vnder truest barres to thrust,
That to my vse it might vn-vsed stay
From hands of falsehood,in sure wards of trust?
But thou,to whom my iewels trifles are,

Most

Most worthy comfort,now my greatest griefe,
Thou best of deerest,and mine onely care,
Art left the prey of euery vulgar theefe.
Thee haue I not lockt vp in any chest,
Saue where thou art not,though I feele thou art,
Within the gentle closure of my brest,
From whence at pleasure thou maist come and part,
 And euen thence thou wilt be stolne I feare,
 For truth prooues theeuish for a prize so deare.

49

AGainst that time (if euer that time come)
 When I shall see thee frowne on my defects,
When as thy loue hath cast his vtmost summe,
Cauld to that audite by aduis'd respects,
Against that time when thou shalt strangely passe,
And scarcely greete me with that sunne thine eye,
When loue conuerted from the thing it was
Shall reasons finde of setled grauitie.
Against that time do I insconce me here
Within the knowledge of mine owne desart,
And this my hand,against my selfe vpreare,
To guard the lawfull reasons on thy part,
 To leaue poore me,thou hast the strength of lawes,
 Since why to loue,I can alledge no cause.

50

HOw heauie doe I iourney on the way,
 When what I seeke (my wearie trauels end)
Doth teach that ease and that repose to say
Thus farre the miles are measurde from thy friend.
The beast that beares me,tired with my woe,
Plods duly on,to beare that waight in me,
As if by some instinct the wretch did know
His rider lou d not speed being made from thee:
The bloody spurre cannot prouoke him on,
That some-times anger thrusts into his hide,
Which heauily he answers with a grone,

D 3

More

More sharpe to me then spurring to his side,
  For that same grone doth put this in my mind,
  My greefe lies onward and my ioy behind.

51

THus can my loue excuse the slow offence,
  Of my dull bearer,when from thee I speed,
From where thou art,why shoulld I hast me thence,
Till I returne of posting is noe need.
O what excuse will my poore beast then find,
When swift extremity can seeme but slow,
Then should I spurre though mounted on the wind,
In winged speed no motion shall I know,
Then can no horse with my desire keepe pace,
Therefore desire(of perfects loue being made)
Shall naigh noe dull flesh in his fiery race,
But loue,for loue,thus shall excuse my iade,
  Since from thee going he went wilfull flow,
  Towards thee ile run,and giue him leaue to goe.

52

SO am I as the rich whose blessed key,
  Can bring him to his sweet vp-locked treasure,
The which he will not eu'ry hower suruay,
For blunting the fine point of seldome pleasure.
Therefore are feasts so sollemne and so rare,
Since sildom comming in the long yeare set,
Like stones of worth they thinly placed are,
Or captaine Iewells in the carconet.
So is the time that keepes you as my chest,
Or as the ward-robe which the robe doth hide,
To make some speciall instant speciall blest,
By new vnfoulding his imprison'd pride.
  Blessed are you whose worthinesse giues skope,
  Being had to tryumph,being lackt to hope.

53

WHat is your substance,whereof are you made,
  That millions of strange shaddowes on you tend?
                Since

Since euery one,hath euery one,one shade,
And you but one,can euery shaddow lend:
Describe *Adonis* and the counterfet,
Is poorely immitated after you,
On *Hellens* cheeke all art of beautie set,
And you in *Grecian* tires are painted new:
Speake of the spring,and foyzon of the yeare,
The one doth shaddow of your beautie show,
The other as your bountie doth appeare,
And you in euery blessed shape we know.
   In all externall grace you haue some part,
   But you like none,none you for constant heart.

54

OH how much more doth beautie beantious seeme,
  By that sweet ornament which truth doth giue,
The Rose lookes faire, but fairer we it deeme
For that sweet odor,which doth in it liue:
The Canker bloomes haue full as deepe a die,
As the perfumed tincture of the Roses,
Hang on such thornes,and play as wantonly,
When sommers breath their masked buds discloses:
But for their virtue only is their show,
They liue vnwoo'd, and vnrespected fade,
Die to themselues . Sweet Roses doe not so,
Of their sweet deathes, are sweetest odors made:
   And so of you,beautious and louely youth,
   When that shall vade,by verse distils your truth.

55

NOt marble, nor the guilded monument,
  Of Princes shall out-liue this powrefull rime,
But you shall shine more bright in these contents
Then vnswept stone, besmeer'd with sluttish time.
When wastefull warre shall *Statues* ouer-turne,
And broiles roote out the worke of masonry,
Nor *Mars* his sword, nor warres quick fire shall burne:
The liuing record of your memory.

                           Gainst

Gainſt death,and all obliuious emnity
Shall you pace forth, your praiſe ſhall ſtil finde roome,
Euen in the eyes of all poſterity
That weare this world out to the ending doome.
  So til the iudgement that your ſelfe ariſe,
  You liue in this,and dwell in louers eies.

56

Sweet loue renew thy force , be it not ſaid
  Thy edge ſhould blunter be then apetite,
Which but too daie by feeding is alaied,
To morrow ſharpned in his former might.
So loue be thou,although too daie thou fil!
Thy hungrie eies,euen till they winck with fulneſſe,
Too morrow ſee againe,and doe not kill
The ſpirit of Loue,with a perpetual dulneſſe:
Let this ſad *Intrim* like the Ocean be
Which parts the ſhore,where two contracted new,
Come daily to the banckes,that when they ſee.
Returne of loue,more bleſt may be the view.
  As cal it Winter,which being ful of care,
  Makes Sōmers welcome,thrice more wiſh'd,more rare .

57

BEing your ſlaue what ſhould I doe but tend,
  Vpon the houres,and times of your deſire?
I haue no precious time at al to ſpend;
Nor ſeruices to doe til you require.
Nor dare I chide the world-without end houre,
Whilſt I(my ſoueraine)watch the clock for you,
Nor thinke the bitterneſſe of abſence ſowre,
VVhen you haue bid your ſeruant once adieue.
Nor dare I queſtion with my iealious thought,
VVhere you may be,or your affaires ſuppoſe,
But like a ſad ſlaue ſtay and thinke of nought
Saue where you are , how happy you make thoſe.
  So true a foole is loue,that in your Will,
  (Though you doe any thing)he thinkes no ill.

58

THat God forbid, that made me first your slaue,
I should in thought controule your times of pleasure,
Or at your hand th' account of houres to craue,
Being your vassail bound to staie your leisure.
Oh let me suffer(being at your beck)
Th' imprison'd absence of your libertie,
And patience tame, to sufferance bide each check,
Without accusing you of iniury.
Be where you list, your charter is so strong,
That you your selfe may priuiledge your time
To what you will, to you it doth belong,
Your selfe to pardon of selfe-doing crime.
   I am to waite, though waiting so be hell,
   Not blame your pleasure be it ill or well.

59

IF their bee nothing new, but that which is,
Hath beene before, how are our braines beguild,
Which laboring for inuention beare amisse
The second burthen of a former child ?
Oh that record could with a back-ward looke,
Euen of fiue hundreth courses of the Sunne,
Show me your image in some antique booke,
Since minde at first in carrecter was done.
That I might see what the old world could say,
To this composed wonder of your frame,
Whether we are mended, or where better they,
Or whether reuolution be the same.
   Oh sure I am the wits of former daies,
   To subiects worse haue giuen admiring praise.

60

LIke as the waues make towards the pibled shore,
So do our minuites hasten to their end,
Each changing place with that which goes before,
In sequent toile all forwards do contend.
Natiuity once in the maine of light.

E   Crawls

Crawles to maturity,wherewith being crown d,
Crooked eclipses gainst his glory fight,
And time that gaue,doth now his gift confound.
Time doth transfixe the florish set on youth,
And delues the paralels in beauties brow,
Feedes on the rarities of natures truth,
And nothing stands but for his sieth to mow.
   And yet to times in hope,my verse shall stand
   Praising thy worth,dispight his cruell hand.

61

IS it thy wil,thy Image should keepe open
My heauy eielids to the weary night?
Dost thou desire my slumbers should be broken,
While shadowes like to thee do mocke my sight?
Is it thy spirit that thou send'st from thee
So farre from home into my deeds to prye,
To find out shames and idle houres in me,
The skope and tenure of thy Ielousie.
O no,thy loue though much,is not so great,
It is my loue that keepes mine eie awake,
Mine owne true loue that doth my rest defeat,
To plaie the watch-man euer for thy sake.
   For thee watch I,whilst thou dost wake elsewhere,
   From me farre of, with others all to neere.

62

SInne of selfe-loue possesseth al mine eie,
And all my soule,and al my euery part;
And for this sinne there is no remedie,
It is so grounded inward in my heart.
Me thinkes no face so gratious is as mine,
No shape so true,no truth of such account,
And for my selfe mine owne worth do define,
As I all other in all worths surmount.
But when my glasse shewes me my selfe indeed
Beated and chopt with tand antiquitie,
Mine owne selfe loue quite contrary I read

Selfe

Selfe,ſo ſelfe louing were iniquity,
　T'is thee(my ſelfe)that for my ſelfe I praiſe,
　Painting my age with beauty of thy daies.

63

AGainſt my loue ſhall be as I am now
　With times iniurious hand chruſht and ore-worne,
When houres haue dreind his blood and fild his brow
With lines and wrincles,when his youthfull morne
Hath trauaild on to Ages ſteepie night,
And all thoſe beauties whereof now he's King
Are vaniſhing,or vaniſht out of ſight,
Stealing away the treaſure of his Spring.
For ſuch a time do I now fortifie
Againſt confounding Ages cruell knife,
That he ſhall neuer cut from memory
My ſweet loues beauty,though my louers life.
　His beautie ſhall in theſe blacke lines be ſeene,
　And they ſhall liue, and he in them ſtill greene.

64

VVHen I haue ſeene by times fell hand defaced
　The rich proud coſt of outworne buried age
When ſometime loftie towers I ſee downe raſed,
And braſſe eternall ſlaue to mortall rage.
When I haue ſeene the hungry Ocean gaine
Aduantage on the Kingdome of the ſhoare,
And the firme ſoile win of the watry maine,
Increaſing ſtore with loſſe,and loſſe with ſtore.
When I haue ſeene ſuch interchange of ſtate,
Or ſtate it ſelfe confounded, to decay,
Ruine hath taught me thus to ruminate
That Time will come and take my loue away.
　This thought is as a death which cannot chooſe
　But weepe to haue,that which it feares to looſe.

65

SInce braſſe,nor ſtone,nor earth,nor boundleſſe ſea,
　But ſad mortallity ore-ſwaies their power,

E 2　　　　　　　　　　　　How

How with this rage shall beautie hold a plea,
Whose action is no stronger then a flower?
O how shall summers hunny breath hold out,
Against the wrackfull siedge of battring dayes,
When rocks impregnable are not so stoute,
Nor gates of steele so strong but time decayes?
O fearefull meditation, where alack,
Shall times best Iewell from times chest lie hid?
Or what strong hand can hold his swift foote back,
Or who his spoile or beautie can forbid?
   O none, vnlesse this miracle haue might,
   That in black inck my loue may still shine bright.

66

TYr'd with all these for restfull death I cry,
  As to behold desert a begger borne,
And needie Nothing trimd in iollitie,
And purest faith vnhappily forsworne,
And gilded honor shamefully misplast,
And maiden vertue rudely strumpeted,
And right perfection wrongfully disgrac'd,
And strength by limping sway disabled,
And arte made tung-tide by authoritie,
And Folly (Doctor-like) controuling skill,
And simple-Truth miscalde Simplicitie,
And captiue-good attending Captaine ill.
   Tyr'd with all these, from these would I be gone,
   Saue that to dye, I leaue my loue alone.

67

AH wherefore with infection should he liue,
  And with his presence grace impietie,
That sinne by him aduantage should atchiue,
And lace it selfe with his societie?
Why should false painting immitate his cheeke,
And steale dead seeing of his liuing hew?
Why should poore beautie indirectly seeke,
Roses of shaddow, since his Rose is true

Why

Why ſhould he liue,now nature banckrout is,
Beggerd of blood to bluſh through liuely vaines,
For ſhe hath no exchecker now but his,
And proud of many,liues vpon his gaines?
　　O him ſhe ſtores,to ſhow what welth ſhe had,
　　In daies long ſince,before theſe laſt ſo bad.

68

THus is his cheeke the map of daies out-worne,
　When beauty liu'd and dy'ed as flowers do now,
Before theſe baſtard ſignes of faire were borne,
Or durſt inhabit on a liuing brow:
Before the goulden treſſes of the dead,
The right of ſepulchers,were ſhorne away,
To liue a ſcond life on ſecond head,
Ere beauties dead fleece made another gay:
In him thoſe holy antique howers are ſeene,
Without all ornament,it ſelfe and true,
Making no ſummer of an others greene,
Robbing no ould to dreſſe his beauty new,
　　And him as for a map doth Nature ſtore,
　　To ſhew faulſe Art what beauty was of yore.

69

THoſe parts of thee that the worlds eye doth view,
　Want nothing that the thought of hearts can mend:
All toungs(the voice of ſoules)giue thee that end,
Vttring bare truth,euen ſo as foes Commend.
Their outward thus with outward praiſe is crownd,
But thoſe ſame toungs that giue thee ſo thine owne,
In other accents doe this praiſe confound
By ſeeing farther then the eye hath ſhowne.
They looke into the beauty of thy mind,
And that in gueſſe they meaſure by thy deeds,
Then churls their thoughts(although their eies were kind)
To thy faire flower ad the rancke ſmell of weeds,
　　But why thy odor matcheth not thy ſhow,
　　The ſolye is this,that thou doeſt common grow.

E 3　　　　　　　　　　That

70

THat thou are blam'd shall not be thy defect,
For slanders marke was euer yet the faire,
The ornament of beauty is suspect,
A Crow that flies in heauens sweetest ayre.
So thou be good, slander doth but approue,
Their worth the greater beeing woo'd of time,
For Canker vice the sweetest buds doth loue,
And thou present'st a pure vnstayined prime.
Thou hast past by the ambush of young daies,
Either not assayld, or victor beeing charg'd,
Yet this thy praise cannot be soe thy praise,
To tye vp enuy, euermore inlarged,
    If some suspect of ill maskt not thy show,
    Then thou alone kingdomes of hearts shouldst owe.

71

NOe Longer mourne for me when I am dead,
Then you shall heare the surly sullen bell
Giue warning to the world that I am fled
From this vile world with vildest wormes to dwell:
Nay if you read this line, remember not,
The hand that writ it, for I loue you so,
That I in your sweet thoughts would be forgot,
If thinking on me then should make you woe.
O if (I say) you looke vpon this verse,
When I (perhaps) compounded am with clay,
Do not so much as my poore name reherse;
But let your loue euen with my life decay.
    Least the wise world should looke into your mone,
    And mocke you with me after I am gon.

72

O Least the world should taske you to recite,
What merit liu'd in me that you should loue
After my death (deare loue) for get me quite,
For you in me can nothing worthy proue.
Vnlesse you would deuise some vertuous lye,

To

To doe more for me then mine owne defert,
And hang more praife vpon deceafed I,
Then nigard truth would willingly impart:
O leaft your true loue may feeme falce in this,
That you for loue fpeake well of me vntrue,
My name be buried where my body is,
And liue no more to fhame nor me, nor you.
   For I am fhamd by that which I bring forth,
   And fo fhould you, to loue things nothing worth.

73

THat time of yeeare thou maift in me behold,
  When yellow leaues, or none, or few doe hange
Vpon thofe boughes which fhake againft the could,
Bare rn'wd quiers, where late the fweet birds fang.
In me thou feeft the twi-light of fuch day,
As after Sun-fet fadeth in the Weft,
Which by and by blacke night doth take away,
Deaths fecond felfe that feals vp all in reft.
In me thou feeft the glowing of fuch fire,
That on the afhes of his youth doth lye,
As the death bed, whereon it muft expire,
Confum'd with that which it was nurrifht by
   This thou perceu'ft, which makes thy loue more ftrong,
   To loue that well, which thou muft leaue ere long.

74

BVt be contented when that fell areft,
  With out all bayle fhall carry me away,
My life hath in this line fome intereft,
Which for memoriall ftill with thee fhall ftay.
When thou reueweft this, thou doeft reuew,
The very part was confecrate to thee,
The earth can haue but earth, which is his due,
My fpirit is thine the better part of me,
So then thou haft but loft the dregs of life,
The pray of wormes, my body being dead,
The coward conqueft of a wretches knife,

To

To bafe of thee to be remembred,
  The worth of that,is that which it containes,
  And that is this, and this with thee remaines.

75

SO are you to my thoughts as food to life,
  Or as fweet feafon'd fhewers are to the ground;
And for the peace of you I hold fuch ftrife,
As twixt a mifer and his wealth is found.
Now proud as an inioyer,and anon
Doubting the filching age will fteale his treafure,
Now counting beft to be with you alone,
Then betterd that the world may fee my pleafure,
Some-time all ful with feafting on your fight,
And by and by cleane ftarued for a looke,
Poffeffing or purfuing no delight
Saue what is had,or muft from you be tooke.
  Thus do I pine and furfet day by day,
  Or gluttoning on all,or all away.

76

VVHy is my verfe fo barren of new pride?
  So far from variation or quicke change?
Why with the time do I not glance afide
To new found methods,and to compounds ftrange?
Why write I ftill all one,euer the fame,
And keepe inuention in a noted weed,
That euery word doth almoft fel my name,
Shewing their birth,and where they did proceed?
O know fweet loue I alwaies write of you,
And you and loue are ftill my argument:
So all my beft is dreffing old words new,
Spending againe what is already fpent:
  For as the Sun is daily new and old,
  So is my loue ftill telling what is told,

77

THy glaffe will fhew thee how thy beauties were,
  Thy dyall how thy pretious mynuits wafte,

The vacant leaues thy mindes imprint will beare,
And of this booke,this learning maift thou tafte.
The wrinckles which thy glaffe will truly fhow,
Of mouthed graues will giue thee memorie,
Thou by thy dyals fhady ftealth maift know,
Times theeuifh progreffe to eternitie.
Looke what thy memorie cannot containe,
Commit to thefe wafte blacks,and thou fhalt finde
Thofe children nurft,deliuerd from thy braine,
To take a new acquaintance of thy minde.
  Thefe offices,fo oft as thou wilt looke,
  Shall profit thee,and much inrich thy booke.

78

SO oft haue I inuok'd thee for my Mufe,
 And found fuch faire affiftance in my verfe,
As euery *Alien* pen hath got my vfe,
And vnder thee their poefie difperfe.
Thine eyes, that taught the dumbe on high to fing,
And heauie ignorance aloft to flie,
Haue added fethers to the learneds wing,
And giuen grace a double Maieftie.
Yet be moft proud of that which I compile,
Whofe influence is thine,and borne of thee,
In others workes thou dooft but mend the ftile,
And Arts with thy fweete graces graced be.
  But thou art al. my art,and dooft aduance
  As high as learning,my rude ignorance.

79

WHilft I alone did call vpon thy ayde,
 My verfe alone had all thy gentle grace,
But now my gracious numbers are decayde,
And my fick Mufe doth giue an other place.
I grant (fweet loue)thy louely argument
Deferues the trauaile of a worthier pen,
Yet what of thee thy Poet doth inuent,
He robs thee of,and payes it thee againe,

F   He

He lends thee vertue,and he ſtole that word,
From thy behauiour,beautie doth he giue
And found it in thy cheeke: he can affoord
No praiſe to thee,but what in thee doth liue.
  Then thanke him not for that which he doth ſay,
  Since what he owes thee,thou thy ſelfe dooſt pay.

80

O How I faint when I of you do write,
  Knowing a better ſpirit doth vſe your name,
And in the praiſe thereof ſpends all his might,
To make me toung-tide ſpeaking of your fame.
But ſince your worth(wide as the Ocean is)
The humble as the proudeſt ſaile doth beare,
My ſawſie barke (inferior farre to his)
On your broad maine doth wilfully appeare.
Your ſhalloweſt helpe will hold me vp a floate,
Whilſt he vpon your ſoundleſſe deepe doth ride,
Or (being wrackt) I am a worthleſſe bote,
He of tall building,and of goodly pride.
  Then If he thriue and I be caſt away,
  The worſt was this,my loue was my decay.

81

OR I ſhall liue your Epitaph to make,
  Or you ſuruiue when I in earth am rotten,
From hence your memory death cannot take,
Although in me each part will be forgotten.
Your name from hence immortall life ſhall haue,
Though I (once gone) to all the world muſt dye,
The earth can yeeld me but a common graue,
When you intombed in mens eyes ſhall lye,
Your monument ſhall be my gentle verſe,
Which eyes not yet created ſhall ore-read,
And toungs to be, your beeing ſhall rehearſe,
When all the breathers of this world are dead,
  You ſtill ſhall liue (ſuch vertue hath my Pen)
  Where breath moſt breaths,euen in the mouths of men.
                                        I grant

82

I Grant thou wert not married to my Mufe,
  And therefore maieſt without attaint ore-looke
The dedicated words which writers vſe
Of their faire ſubieĉt,bleſſing euery booke.
Thou art as faire in knowledge as in hew,
Finding thy worth a limmit paſt my praiſe,
And therefore art inſorc'd to ſeeke anew,
Some freſher ſtampe of the time bettering dayes.
And do ſo loue,yet when they haue deuiſde,
What ſtrained touches Rhethorick can lend,
Thou truly faire,wert truly ſimpathizde,
In true plaine words ,by thy true telling friend.
  And their groſſe painting might be better vſ'd,
  Where cheekes need blood,in thee it is abuſ'd.

83

I Neuer ſaw that you did painting need,
  And therefore to your faire no painting ſet,
I found (or thought I found) you did exceed,
The barren tender of a Poets debt :
And therefore haue I ſlept in your report,
That you your ſelfe being extant well might ſhow,
How farre a moderne quill doth come to ſhort,
Speaking of worth,what worth in you doth grow,
This ſilence for my ſinne you did impute,
Which ſhall be moſt my glory being dombe,
For I impaire not beautie being mute,
When others would giue life,and bring a tombe.
  There liues more life in one of your faire eyes,
  Then both your Poets can in praiſe deuiſe.

84

WHo is it that ſayes moſt,which can ſay more,
  Then this rich praiſe,that you alone,are you,
In whoſe confine immured is the ſtore,
Which ſhould example where your equall grew,
Leane penurie within that Pen doth dwell,

That

That to his subiect lends not some small glory,
But he that writes of you,if he can tell,
That you are you,so dignifies his story.
Let him but coppy what in you is writ,
Not making worse what nature made so cleere,
And such a counter-part shall fame his wit,
Making his stile admired euery where.
   You to your beautious blessings adde a curse,
   Being fond on praise,which makes your praises worse.

85

MY toung-tide Muse in manners holds her still,
  While comments of your praise richly compil'd,
Reserue their Character with goulden quill,
And precious phrase by all the Muses fil'd.
I thinke good thoughts,whilst other write good wordes,
And like vnlettered clarke still crie Amen,
To euery Himne that able spirit affords,
In polisht forme of well refined pen.
Hearing you praisd,I say 'tis so, 'tis true,
And to the most of praise adde some-thing more,
But that is in my thought,whose loue to you
(Though words come hind-most)holds his ranke before.
   Then others,for the breath of words respect,
   Me for my dombe thoughts,speaking in effect.

86

VVAs it the proud full saile of his great verse,
  Bound for the prize of (all to precious) you,
That did my ripe thoughts in my braine inhearce,
Making their tombe the wombe wherein they grew?
Was it his spirit,by spirits taught to write,
Aboue a mortall pitch,that struck me dead?
No,neither he,nor his compiers by night
Giuing him ayde,my verse astonished.
He nor that affable familiar ghost
Which nightly gulls him with intelligence,
As victors of my silence cannot boast,

I was

I was not sick of any feare from thence,
　But when your countinance fild vp his line,
　Then lackt I matter, that infeebled mine.

87

FArewell thou art too deare for my posseffing,
　Ard like enough thou knowft thy eftimate,
The Cha.ter of thy worth giues thee releasing:
My bor.ds in thee are all determinate.
For how do I hold thee but by thy granting,
And for that ritches where is my deseruing?
The caufe of this faire guift in me is wanting,
And fo my pattent back againe is fweruing.
Thy felfe thou gau'ft, thy owne worth then not knowing,
Or mee to whom thou gau'ft it, elfe miftaking,
So thy great guift vpon mifprifion growing,
Comes home againe, on better iudgement making.
　　Thus haue I had thee as a dreame doth flatter,
　　In fleepe a King, but waking no fuch matter.

88

VVHen thou fhalt be difpode to fet me light,
　　And place my merrit in the eie of skorne,
Vpon thy fide, againft my felfe ile fight,
And proue thee virtuous, though thou art forfworne:
With mine owne weakeneffe being beft acquainted,
Vpon thy part I can fet downe a ftory
Of faults conceald, wherein I am attainted :
That thou in loofing me fhall win much glory.
And I by this wil be a gainer too,
For bending all my louing thoughts on thee,
The iniuries that to my felfe I doe,
Doing thee vantage, duble vantage me.
　　Such is my loue, to thee I fo belong,
　　That for thy right, my felfe will beare all wrong.

89

SAy that thou didft forfake mee for fome falt,
　And I will comment vpon that offence,

F 3　　　　　　　　　　　　　The

ſpeake of my lameneſſe, and I ſtraight will halt:
Againſt thy reaſons making no defence.
Thou canſt not(loue)diſgrace me halfe ſo ill,
To ſet a forme vpon deſired change,
As ile my ſelfe diſgrace,knowing thy wil,
I will acquaintance ſtrangle and looke ſtrange:
Be abſent from thy walkes and in my tongue,
Thy ſweet beloued name no more ſhall dwell,
Leaſt I(too much prophane)ſhould do it wronge:
And haplie of our old acquaintance tell.
   For thee,againſt my ſelfe ile vow debate,
   For I muſt nere loue him whom thou doſt hate.

90

THen hate me when thou wilt, if euer,now,
  Now while the world is bent my deeds to croſſe,
Ioyne with the ſpight of fortune,make me bow,
And doe not drop in for an after loſſe:
Ah doe not,when my heart hath ſcapte this ſorrow,
Come in the rereward of a conquerd woe,
Giue not a windy night a rainie morrow,
To linger out a purpoſd ouer-throw.
If thou wilt leaue me, do not leaue me laſt,
When other pettie griefes haue done their ſpight,
But in the onſet come,ſo ſtall I taſte
At firſt the very worſt of fortunes might.
   And other ſtraines of woe, which now ſeeme woe,
   Compar'd with loſſe of thee,will not ſeeme ſo.

91

SOme glory in their birth,ſome in their skill,
  Some in their wealth, ſome in their bodies force,
Some in their garments though new-fangled ill:
Some in their Hawkes and Hounds,ſome in their Horſe.
And euery humor hath his adiunct pleaſure,
Wherein it findes a ioy aboue the reſt,
But theſe perticulers are not my meaſure,
All theſe I better in one generall beſt.

Thy

Thy loue is bitter then high birth to me,
Richer then wealth, prouder then garments coſt,
Of more delight then Hawkes or Horſes bee:
And hauing chee, of all mens pride I boaſt.
    Wretched in this alone, that thou maiſt take,
    All this away, and me moſt wretched make.

92

BVt doe thy worſt to ſteale thy ſelfe away,
  For tearme of life thou art aſſured mine,
And life no longer then thy loue will ſtay,
For it depends vpon that loue of thine.
Then need I not to feare the worſt of wrongs,
When in the leaſt of them my life hath end,
I ſee, a better ſtate to me belongs
Then that, which on thy humor doth depend.
Thou canſt not vex me with inconſtant minde,
Since that my life on thy reuolt doth lie,
Oh what a happy title do I finde,
Happy to haue thy loue, happy to die!
    But whats ſo bleſſed faire that feares no blot,
    Thou maiſt be falce, and yet I know it not.

93

SO ſhall I liue, ſuppoſing thou art true,
  Like a deceiued husband, ſo loues face,
May ſtill ſeeme loue to me, though alter'd new:
Thy lookes with me, thy heart in other place.
For their can liue no hatred in thine eye,
Therefore in that I cannot know thy change,
In manies lookes, the falce hearts hiſtory
Is writ in moods and frounes and wrinckles ſtrange.
But heauen in thy creation did decree,
That in thy face ſweet loue ſhould euer dwell,
What ere thy thoughts, or thy hearts workings be,
Thy lookes ſhould nothing thence, but ſweetneſſe tell,
    How like *Eaues* apple doth thy beauty grow,
    If thy ſweet vertue anſwere not thy ſhow.

94

THey that haue powre to hurt, and will doe none,
That doe not do the thing, they moſt do ſhowe,
Who mouing others, are themſelues as ſtone,
Vnmooued, could, and to temptation ſlow:
They rightly do inherrit heauens graces,
And husband natures ritches from expence,
They are the Lords and owners of their faces,
Others, but ſtewards of their excellence:
The ſommers ſlowre is to the ſommer ſweet,
Though to it ſelfe, it onely liue and die,
But if that flowre with baſe infection meete,
The baſeſt weed out-braues his dignity:
　　For ſweeteſt things turne ſowreſt by their deedes,
　　Lillies that feſter, ſmell far worſe then weeds.

95

HOw ſweet and louely doſt thou make the ſhame,
Which like a canker in the fragrant Roſe,
Doth ſpot the beautie of thy budding name?
Oh in what ſweets doeſt thou thy ſinnes incloſe!
That tongue that tells the ſtory of thy daies,
(Making laſciuious comments on thy ſport)
Cannot diſpraiſe, but in a kinde of praiſe,
Naming thy name, bleſſes an ill report.
Oh what a manſion haue thoſe vices got,
Which for their habitation choſe out thee,
Where beauties vaile doth couer euery blot,
And all things turnes to faire, that eies can ſee!
　　Take heed (deare heart) of this large priuiledge,
　　The hardeſt knife ill vſ'd doth looſe his edge.

96

SOme ſay thy fault is youth, ſome wantoneſſe,
Some ſay thy grace is youth and gentle ſport,
Both grace and faults are lou'd of more and leſſe:
Thou makſt faults graces, that to thee reſort:
As on the finger of a throned Queene,

The

The baseſt Iewell wil be well eſteem'd:
So are thoſe errors that in thee are ſeene,
To truths tranſlated,and for true things deem'd.
How many Lambs might the ſterne Wolfe betray,
If like a Lambe he could his lookes tranſlate.
How many gazers mighſt thou lead away,
If thou wouldſt vſe the ſtrength of all thy ſtate?
　　But doe not ſo,I loue thee in ſuch ſort,
　　As thou being mine,mine is thy good report.

97

HOw like a Winter hath my abſence beene
From thee,the pleaſure of the fleeting yeare?
　　What freezings haue I felt,what darke daies ſeene?
What old Decembers bareneſſe euery where?
And yet this time remou'd was ſommers time,
The teeming Autumne big with ritch increaſe,
Bearing the wanton burthen of the prime,
Like widdowed wombes after their Lords deceaſe:
Yet this aboundant iſſue ſeem'd to me,
But hope of Orphans,and vn-fathered fruite,
For Sommer and his pleaſures waite on thee,
And thou away,the very birds are mute.
　　Or if they ſing,tis with ſo dull a cheere,
　　That leaues looke pale,dreading the Winters neere.

98

FRom you haue I beene abſent in the ſpring,
When proud pide Aprill (dreſt in all his trim)
Hath put a ſpirit of youth in euery thing:
That heauie *Saturne* laught and leapt with him.
Yet nor the laies of birds,nor the ſweet ſmell
Of different flowers in odor and in hew,
Could make me any ſummers ſtory tell:
Or from their proud lap pluck them where they grew:
Nor did I wonder at the Lillies white,
Nor praiſe the deepe vermillion in the Roſe,
They weare but ſweet,but figures of delight:
　　　　　　　G　　　　　　　　　Drawne

Drawne after you, you patterne of all those.
 Yet seem'd it Winter still, and you away,
 As with your shaddow I with these did play.

99

THe forward violet thus did I chide,
 Sweet theese whence didst thou steale thy sweet that
If not from my loues breath, the purple pride,   (smels
Which on thy soft checke for complexion dwells?
In my loues veines thou hast too grosely died,
The Lillie I condemned for thy hand,
And buds of marierom had stolne thy haire,
The Roses fearefully on thornes did stand,
Our blushing shame, an other white dispaire:
A third nor red, nor white, had stolne of both,
And to his robbry had annext thy breath,
But for his theft in pride of all his growth
A vengfull canker eate him vp to death.
  More flowers I noted, yet I none could see,
  But sweet, or culler it had stolne from thee.

100

VVHere art thou Muse that thou forgetst so long,
 To speake of that which giues thee all thy might?
Spendst thou thy furie on some worthlesse songe,
Darkning thy powre to lend base subiects light,
Returne forgetfull Muse, and straight redeeme,
In gentle numbers time so idely spent,
Sing to the eare that doth thy laies esteeme,
And giues thy pen both skill and argument.
Rise resty Muse, my loues sweet face suruay,
If time haue any wrincle grauen there,
If any, be a *Satire* to decay,
And make times spoiles dispised euery where.
  Giue my loue fame faster then time wasts life,
  So thou preuenst his sieth, and crooked knife,

101

OH truant Muse what shalbe thy amends,

For

For thy neglect of truth in beauty di'd?
Both truth and beauty on my loue depends:
So dost thou too,and therein dignifi'd:
Make answere Muse,wilt thou not haply saie,
Truth needs no collour with his collour fixt,
Beautie no pensell,beauties truth to lay:
But best is best,if neuer intermixt.
Because he needs no praise,wilt thou be dumb?
Excuse not silence so,for't lies in thee,
To make him much out-liue a gilded tombe:
And to be prais'd of ages yet to be.
    Then do thy office Muse,I teach thee how,
    To make him seeme long hence,as he showes now.

102

MY loue is strengthned though more weake in see-
I loue not lesse,thogh lesse the show appeare, (ming
That loue is marchandiz'd,whose ritch esteeming,
The owners tongue doth publish euery where.
Our loue was new,and then but in the spring,
When I was wont to greet it with my laies,
As *Philomell* in summers front doth singe,
And stops his pipe in growth of riper daies:
Not that the summer is lesse pleasant now
Then when her mournefull himns did hush the night,
But that wild musick burthens euery bow,
And sweets growne common loose their deare delight.
    Therefore like her,I some-time hold my tongue:
    Because I would not dull you with my songe.

103

ALack what pouerty my Muse brings forth,
That hauing such a skope to show her pride,
The argument all bare is of more worth
Then when it hath my added praise beside.
Oh blame me not if I no more can write!
Looke in your glasse and there appeares a face,
That ouer-goes my blunt inuention quite,
Dulling my lines,and doing me disgrace.

                    Were

Were it not sinfull then striuing to mend,
To marre the subiect that before was well,
For to no other passe my verses tend,
Then of your graces and your gifts to tell.
   And more,much more then in my verse can sit,
   Your owne glasse showes you,when you looke in it.

104

TO me faire friend you neuer can be old,
  For as you were when first your eye I eyde,
Such seemes your beautie still:Three Winters colde,
Haue from the forrests shooke three summers pride,
Three beautious springs to yellow *Autumne* turn'd,
In processe of the seasons haue I seene,
Three Aprill perfumes in three hot Iunes burn'd,
Since first I saw you fresh which yet are greene.
Ah yet doth beauty like a Dyall hand,
Steale from his figure,and no pace perceiu'd,
So your sweete hew,which me thinkes still doth stand,
Hath motion,and mine eye may be deceaued.
   For feare of which,heare this thou age vnbred,
   Ere you were borne was beauties summer dead.

105

LEt not my loue be cal'd Idolatrie,
  Nor my beloued as an Idoll show,
Since all alike my songs and praises be
To one,of one,still such,and euer so.
Kinde is my loue to day,to morrow kinde,
Still constant in a wondrous excellence,
Therefore my verse to constancie confin'de,
One thing expressing,leaues out difference.
Faire,kinde,and true,is all my argument,
Faire,kinde and true,varrying to other words,
And in this change is my inuention spent,
Three theams in one,which wondrous scope affords.
   Faire,kinde,and true,haue often liu'd alone.
   Which three till now,neuer kept seate in one.

When

106

WHen in the Chronicle of wasted time,
  I see discriptions of the fairest wights,
And beautie making beautifull old rime,
In praise of Ladies dead,and louely Knights,
Then in the blazon of sweet beauties best,
Of hand,of foote,of lip,of eye,of brow,
I see their antique Pen would haue exprest,
Euen such a beauty as you maister now.
So all their praises are but prophesies
Of this our time,all you prefiguring,
And for they look'd but with deuining eyes,
They had not still enough your worth to sing :
  For we which now behold these present dayes,
  Haue eyes to wonder,but lack toungs to praise.

107

NOt mine owne feares,nor the prophetick soule,
  Of the wide world,dreaming on things to come,
Can yet the lease of my true loue controule,
Supposde as forfeit to a confin'd doome.
The mortall Moone hath her eclipse indur'de,
And the sad Augurs mock their owne presage,
Incertenties now crowne them-selues assur'de,
And peace proclaimes Oliues of endlesse age.
Now with the drops of this most balmie time,
My loue lookes fresh,and death to me subscribes,
Since spight of him Ile liue in this poore rime,
While he insults ore dull and speachlesse tribes.
  And thou in this shalt finde thy monument,
  When tyrants crests and tombs of brasse are spent.

108

VVHat's in the braine that Inck may character,
  Which hath not figur'd to thee my true spirit,
What's new to speake,what now to register,
That may expresse my loue,or thy deare merit ?
Nothing sweet boy,but yet like prayers diuine,
G 3   I must

I must each day say ore the very same,
Counting no old thing old, thou mine, I thine,
Euen as when first I hallowed thy faire name.
So that eternall loue in loues fresh case,
Waighes not the dust and iniury of age,
Nor giues to necessary wrinckles place,
But makes antiquitie for aye his page,
   Finding the first conceit of loue there bred,
   Where time and outward forme would shew it dead,

109

O Neuer say that I was false of heart,
  Though absence seem'd my flame to quallifie,
As easie might I from my selfe depart,
As from my soule which in thy brest doth lye:
That is my home of loue, if I haue rang'd,
Like him that trauels I returne againe,
Iust to the time, not with the time exchang'd,
So that my selfe bring water for my staine,
Neuer beleeue though in my nature raign'd,
All frailties that besiege all kindes of blood,
That it could so preposterouslie be stain'd,
To leaue for nothing all thy summe of good:
   For nothing this wide Vniuerse I call,
   Saue thou my Rose, in it thou art my all.

110

A Las 'tis true, I haue gone here and there,
  And made my selfe a motley to the view,
Gor'd mine own thoughts, sold cheap what is most deare,
Made old offences of affections new.
Most true it is, that I haue lookt on truth
Asconce and strangely: But by all aboue,
These blenches gaue my heart an other youth,
And worse essaies prou'd thee my best of loue,
Now all is done, haue what shall haue no end,
Mine appetite I neuer more will grin'de
On newer proofe, to trie an older friend,
A God in loue, to whom I am confin'd.

Then

Then giue me welcome, next my heauen the beft,
Euen to thy pure and moft moft louing breft.

111

O For my fake doe you wifh fortune chide,
    The guiltie goddeffe of my harmfull deeds,
That did not better for my life prouide,
Then publick meanes which publick manners breeds.
Thence comes it that my name receiues a brand,
And almoft thence my nature is fubdu'd
To what it workes in, like the Dyers hand,
Pitty me then, and wifh I were renu'de,
Whilft like a willing pacient I will drinke,
Potions of Eyfell gainft my ftrong infection,
No bitterneffe that I will bitter thinke,
Nor double pennance to correct correction.
    Pittie me then deare friend, and I affure yee,
    Euen that your pittie is enough to cure mee.

112

YOur loue and pittie doth th'impreffion fill,
    Which vulgar fcandall ftampt vpon my brow,
For what care I who calles me well or ill,
So you ore-greene my bad, my good alow?
You are my All the world, and I muft ftriue,
To know my fhames and praifes from your tounge,
None elfe to me, nor I to none aliue,
That my fteel'd fence or changes right or wrong,
In fo profound *Abifme* I throw all care
Of others voyces, that my Adders fence,
To cryttick and to flatterer ftopped are:
Marke how with my neglect I doe difpence.
    You are fo ftrongly in my purpofe bred,
    That all the world befides me thinkes y'are dead.

113

SInce I left you, mine eye is in my minde,
    And that which gouernes me to goe about,
Doth part his function, and is partly blind,

Seemes

Seemes seeing, but effectually is out:
For it no forme deliuers to the heart
Of bird, of flowre, or shape which it doth lack,
Of his quick obiects hath the minde no part,
Nor his owne vision houlds what it doth catch:
For if it see the rud'st or gentlest sight,
The most sweet-fauor or deformedst creature,
The mountaine, or the sea, the day, or night:
The Croe, or Doue, it shapes them to your feature.
   Incapable of more repleat, with you,
   My most true minde thus maketh mine vntrue.

114

OR whether doth my minde being crown'd with you
Drinke vp the monarks plague this flattery?
Or whether shall I say mine eie saith true,
And that your loue taught it this *Alcumie*?
To make of monsters, and things indigest,
Such cherubines as your sweet selfe resemble,
Creating euery bad a perfect best
As fast as obiects to his beames assemble:
Oh tis the first, tis flatry in my seeing,
And my great minde most kingly drinkes it vp,
Mine eie well knowes what with his gust is greeing,
And to his pallat doth prepare the cup.
   If it be poison'd, tis the lesser sinne,
   That mine eye loues it and doth first beginne.

115

THose lines that I before haue writ doe lie,
Euen those that said I could not loue you deerer,
Yet then my iudgement knew no reason why,
My most full flame should afterwards burne cleerer.
But reckening time, whose milliond accidents
Creepe in twixt vowes, and change decrees of Kings,
Tan sacred beautie, blunt the sharp'st intents,
Diuert strong mindes to th'course of altring things:
Alas why fearing of times tiranie,

             Might

Might I not then say now I loue you best,
When I was certaine ore in-certainty,
Crowning the present,doubting of the rest:
    Loue is a Babe , then might I not say so
    To giue full growth to that which still doth grow.

119

LEt me not to the marriage of true mindes
    Admit impediments,loue is not loue
Which alters when it alteration findes,
Or bends with the remouer to remoue.
O no,it is an euer fixed marke
That lookes on tempests and is neuer shaken;
It is the star to euery wandring barke,
Whose worths vnknowne,although his higth be taken.
Lou's not Times foole,though rosie lips and cheeks
Within his bending sickles compasse come,
Loue alters not with his breese houres and weekes,
But beares it out euen to the edge of doome:
    If this be error and vpon me proued,
    I neuer writ,nor no man euer loued.

117

ACcuse me thus,that I haue scanted all,
    Wherein I should your great deserts repay,
Forgot vpon your dearest loue to call,
Where o al bonds do tie me day by day,
That I haue frequent binne with vnknown mindes,
And giuen to time your owne deare purchas'd right,
That I haue hoysted saile to al the windes
Which should transport me farthest from your sight.
Booke both my wilfulnesse and errors downe,
And on iust proofe surmise,accumilate,
Bring me within the leuel of your frowne,
But shoote not at me in your wakened hate:
    Since my appeale saies I did striue to prooue
    The constancy and virtue of your loue

118

Like as to make our appetites more keene
With eager compounds we our pallat vrge,
As to preuent our malladies vnseene,
We sicken to shun sicknesse when we purge.
Euen so being full of your nere cloying sweetnesse,
To bitter sawces did I frame my feeding;
And sicke of wel-fare found a kind of meetnesse,
To be diseas'd ere that there was true needing.
Thus pollicie in loue t'anticipate
The ills that were,not grew to faults assured,
And brought to medicine a healthfull state
Which rancke of goodnesse would by ill be cured.
　　But thence I learne and find the lesson true,
　　Drugs poyson him that so fell sicke of you.

119

What potions haue I drunke of *Syren* teares
Distil'd from Lymbecks foule as hell within,
Applying feares to hopes,and hopes to feares,
Still loosing when I saw my selfe to win?
What wretched errors hath my heart committed,
Whilst it hath thought it selfe so blessed neuer?
How haue mine eies out of their Spheares bene fitted
In the distraction of this madding feuer?
O benefit of ill, now I find true
That better is, by euil still made better.
And ruin'd loue when it is built anew
Growes fairer then at first,more strong,far greater.
　　So I returne rebukt to my content,
　　And gaine by ills thrise more then I haue spent.

120

That you were once vnkind be-friends mee now,
And for that sorrow , which I then didde feele,
Needes must I vnder my transgression bow,
Vnlesse my Nerues were brasse or hammered steele.
For if you were by my vnkindnesse shaken

As

As I by yours , y'haue paſt a hell of Time,
And I a tyrant haue no leaſure taken
To waigh how once I ſuffered in your crime.
O that our night of wo might haue remembred
My deepeſt ſence,how hard true ſorrow hits,
And ſoone to you,as you to me then tendred
The humble ſalue,which wounded boſomes fits!
    But that your treſpaſſe now becomes a fee,
    Mine ranſoms yours,and yours muſt ranſome mee,

121

TIS better to be vile then vile eſteemed,
   When not to be,receiues reproach of being,
And the iuſt pleaſure loſt,which is ſo deemed,
Not by our feeling,but by others ſeeing.
For why ſhould others falſe adulterat eyes
Giue ſalutation to my ſportiue blood?
Or on my frailties why are frailer ſpies;
Which in their wils count bad what I think good?
Noe, I am that I am,and they that leuell
At my abuſes,reckon vp their owne,
I may be ſtraight though they them-ſelues be beuel
By their rancke thoughtes,my deedes muſt not be ſhown
    Vnleſſe this generall euill they maintaine,
    All men are bad and in their badneſſe raigne.

122.

THy guifts,,thy tables,are within my braine
   Full characterd with laſting memory,
Which ſhall aboue that idle rancke remaine
Beyond all date euen to eternity.
Or at the leaſt,ſo long as braine and heart
Haue facultie by nature to ſubſiſt,
Til each to raz'd obliuion yeeld his part
Of thee,thy record neuer can be miſt:
That poore retention could not ſo much hold,
Nor need I tallies thy deare loue to skore,
Therefore to giue them from me was I bold,

To truſt thoſe tables that receaue thee more,
   To keepe an adiunckt to remember thee,
   Were to import forgetfulneſſe in mee.

123

NO! Time, thou ſhalt not boſt that I doe change,
   Thy pyramyds buylt vp with newer might
To me are nothing nouell, nothing ſtrange,
They are but dreſſings of a former ſight:
Our dates are breeſe, and therefor we admire,
What thou doſt foyſt vpon vs that is ould,
And rather make them borne to our deſire,
Then thinke that we before haue heard them tould:
Thy regiſters and thee I both defie,
Not wondring at the preſent, nor the paſt,
For thy records, and what we ſee doth lye,
Made more or les by thy continuall haſt:
   This I doe vow and this ſhall euer be,
   I will be true diſpight thy ſyeth and thee.

124

YF my deare loue were but the childe of ſtate,
   It might for fortunes baſterd be vnfathered,
As ſubiect to times loue, or to times hate,
Weeds among weeds, or flowers with flowers gatherd.
No it was buylded far from accident,
It ſuffers not in ſmilinge pomp, nor falls
Vnder the blow of thralled diſcontent,
Whereto th'inuiting time our faſhion calls:
It feares not policy that *Hereticke*,
Which workes on leaſes of ſhort numbred howers,
But all alone ſtands hugely pollitick,
That it nor growes with heat, nor drownes with ſhowres.
   To this I witnes call the foles of time,
   Which die for goodnes, who haue liu'd for crime.

125

VVEr't ought to me I bore the canopy,
   With my extern the ourward honoring,

Or

Or layd great bases for eternity,
Which proues more short then wast or ruining?
Haue I not seene dwellers on forme and fauor
Lose all, and more by paying too much rent
For compound sweet; Forgoing simple sauor,
Pittifull thriuors in their gazing spent.
Noe, let me be obsequious in thy heart,
And take thou my oblacion, poore but free,
Which is not mixt with seconds, knows no art,
But mutuall render onely me for thee.

    Hence, thou subbornd *Informer*, a trew soule
    When most impeacht, stands least in thy controule.

126

O Thou my louely Boy who in thy power,
  Doest hould times fickle glasse, his fickle, hower:
Who hast by wayning growne, and therein shou'st,
Thy louers withering, as thy sweet selfe grow'st.
If Nature (soueraine misteres ouer wrack)
As thou goest onwards still will plucke thee backe,
She keepes thee to this purpose, that her skill.
May time disgrace, and wretched mynuit kill.
Yet feare her O thou minnion of her pleasure,
She may detaine, but not still keepe her tresure!
Her *Audite* (though delayd) answer'd must be,
And her *Quietus* is to render thee.

    (   )
    (   )

127

IN the ould age blacke was not counted faire,
Or if it weare it bore not beauties name:
But now is blacke beauties successiue heire,
And Beautie slanderd with a bastard shame,
For since each hand hath put on Natures power,
Fairing the foule with Arts faulse borrow'd face,
Sweet beauty hath no name no holy boure,
But is prophan'd, if not liues in disgrace.

H 3   Therefore

Therefore my Mistersse eyes are Rauen blacke,
Her eyes so suted, and they mourners seeme,
At such who not borne faire no beauty lack,
Slandring Creation with a false esteeme,
   Yet so they mourne becomming of their woe,
   That euery toung saies beauty should looke so.

128

HOw oft when thou my musike musike playst,
  Vpon that blessed wood whose motion sounds
With thy sweet fingers when thou gently swayst,
The wiry concord that mine eare confounds,
Do I enuie those Iackes that nimble leape,
To kisse the tender inward of thy hand,
Whilst my poore lips which should that haruest reape,
At the woods bouldnes by thee blushing stand.
To be so tikled they would change their state,
And situation with those dancing chips,
Ore whome their fingers walke with gentle gate,
Making dead wood more blest then liuing lips,
   Since sausie Iackes so happy are in this,
   Giue them their fingers, me thy lips to kisse.

129

TH'expence of Spirit in a waste of shame
  Is lust in action, and till action , lust
Is periurd, murdrous, blouddy full of blame,
Sauage, extreame, rude, cruell, not to trust,
Inioyd no sooner but dispised straight,
Past reason hunted, and no sooner had
Past reason hated as a swollowed bayt,
On purpose layd to make the taker mad.
Made In pursut and in possession so,
Had, hauing, and in quest, to haue extreame,
A blisse in proofe and proud and very wo,
Before a ioy proposd behind a dreame,
   All this the world well knowes yet none knowes well,
   To shun the heauen that leads men to this hell.

                          My

130

MY Miſtres eyes are nothing like the Sunne,
Currall is farre more red,then her lips red,
If ſnow be white,why then her breſts are dun:
It haires be wiers,black wiers grow on her head:
I haue ſeene Roſes damaskt,red and white,
But no ſuch Roſes ſee I in her cheekes,
And in ſome perfumes is there more delight,
Then in the breath that from my Miſtres reekes.
I loue to heare her ſpeake,yet well I know,
That Muſicke hath a farre   more pleaſing ſound:
I graunt I neuer ſaw a goddeſſe goe,
My Miſtres when ſhee walkes treads on the ground.
     And yet by heauen I thinke my loue as rare,
     As any ſhe beli'd with falſe compare.

131

THou art as tiranous,ſo as thou art,
As thoſe whoſe beauties proudly make them cruell
For well thou know'ſt to my deare doting hart
Thou art the faireſt and moſt precious Iewell.
Yet in good faith ſome ſay that thee behold,
Thy face hath not the power to make loue grone;
To ſay they erre,I dare not be ſo bold,
Although I ſweare it to my ſelfe alone.
And to be ſure that is not falſe I ſweare
A thouſand grones but thinking on thy face,
One on anothers necke do witneſſe beare
Thy blacke is faireſt in my iudgements place.
     In nothing art thou blacke ſaue in thy deeds,
     And thence this ſlaunder as I thinke proceeds.

132

THine eies I loue,and they as pittying me,
Knowing thy heart torment me with diſdaine,
Haue put on black,and louing mourners bee,
Looking with pretty ruth vpon my paine,

And

And truly not the morning Sun of Heauen
Better becomes the gray cheeks of th' East,
Nor that full Starre that vshers in the Eauen
Doth halfe that glory to the sober West
As those two morning eyes become thy face:
O let it then as well beseeme thy heart
To mourne for me since mourning doth thee grace,
And sute thy pitty like in euery part.
   Then will I sweare beauty her selfe is blacke,
   And all they foule that thy complexion lacke.

133

BEshrew that heart that makes my heart to groane
For that deepe wound it giues my friend and me;
I'st not ynough to torture me alone,
But slaue to slauery my sweet'st friend must be.
Me from my selfe thy cruell eye hath taken,
And my next selfe thou harder hast ingrossed,
Of him,my selfe,and thee I am forsaken,
A torment thrice three-fold thus to be crossed :
Prison my heart in thy steele bosomes warde,
But then my friends heart let my poore heart bale,
Who ere keepes me,let my heart be his garde,
Thou canst not then vse rigor in my Iaile.
   And yet thou wilt,for I being pent in thee,
   Perforce am thine and all that is in me.

134

SO now I haue confest that he is thine,
And I my selfe am morgag'd to thy will,
My selfe Ile forfeit,so that other mine,
Thou wilt restore to be my comfort still:
But thou wilt not,nor he will not be free,
For thou art couetous,and he is kinde,
He learnd but suretie-like to write for me,
Vnder that bond that him as fast doth binde.
The statute of thy beauty thou wilt take,
Thou vsurer that put'st forth all to vse,

And sue a friend,came debter for my sake,
So him I loose through my vnkinde abuse.
   Him haue I lost,thou hast both him and me,
   He paies the whole,and yet am I not free.

135

WHo euer hath her wish,thou hast thy *Will*,
   And *Will* too boote,and *Will* in ouer-plus,
More then enough am I that vexe thee still,
To thy sweet will making addition thus.
Wilt thou whose will is large and spatious,
Not once vouchsafe to hide my will in thine,
Shall will in others seeme right gracious,
And in my will no faire acceptance shine:
The sea all water,yet receiues raine still,
And in aboundance addeth to his store,
So thou beeing rich in *Will* adde to thy *Will*,
One will of mine to make thy large *Will* more.
   Let no vnkinde,no faire beseechers kill,
   Thinke all but one,and me in that one *Will*.

136

IF thy soule check thee that I come so neere,
   Sweare to thy blind soule that I was thy *Will*,
And will thy soule knowes is admitted there,
Thus farre for loue, my loue-sure sweet fullfill.
Will, will fulfill the treasure of thy loue,
I fill it full with wils,and my will one,
In things of great receit with ease we prooue,
Among a number one is reckon'd none.
Then in the number let me passe vntold,
Though in thy stores account I one must be,
For nothing hold me so it please thee hold,
That nothing me,a some-thing sweet to thee.
   Make but my name thy loue,and loue that still,
   And then thou louest me for my name is *Will*.

137

THou blinde foole loue,what doost thou to mine eyes,
                      I   That

That they behold and fee not what they fee :
They know what beautie is,fee where it lyes,
Yet what the beft is,take the worft to be.
If eyes corrupt by ouer-partiall lookes,
Be anchord in the baye where all men ride,
Why of eyes falfehood haft thou forged hookes.
Whereto the iudgement of my heart is tide?
Why fhould my heart thinke that a feuerall plot,
Which my heart knowes the wide worlds common place?
Or mine eyes feeing this,fay this is not
To put faire truth vpon fo foule a face,
      In things right true my heart and eyes haue erred,
      And to this falfe plague are they now tranfferred.

138

WHen my loue fweares that fhe is made of truth,
      I do beleeue her though I know fhe lyes,
That fhe might thinke me fome vntuterd youth,
Vnlearned in the worlds falfe fubtilties.
Thus vainely thinking that fhe thinkes me young,
Although fhe knowes my dayes are paft the beft,
Simply I credit her falfe fpeaking tongue,
On both fides thus is fimple truth fupprest :
But wherefore fayes fhe not fhe is vniuft ?
And wherefore fay not I that I am old?
O loues beft habit is in feeming truft,
And age in loue,loues not t'haue yeares told.
      Therefore I lye with her,and fhe with me,
      And in our faults by lyes we flattered be.

139

OCall not me to iuftifie the wrong,
      I hat thy vnkindneffe layes vpon my heart,
Wound me not with thine eye but with thy toung.
Vfe power with power,and flay me not by Art,
Tell me thou lou'ft elfe-where;but in my fight,
Deare heart forbeare to glance thine eye afide,
What needft thou wound with cunning when thy might

Is more then my ore-preſt defence can bide?
Let me excuſe thee ah my loue well knowes,
Her prettie lookes haue beene mine enemies,
And therefore from my face ſhe turnes my foes,
That they elſe-where might dart their iniuries :
   Yet do not ſo,but ſince I am neere ſlaine,
   Kill me out-right with lookes,and rid my paine.

140

BE wiſe as thou art cruell,do not preſſe
  My toung tide patience with too much diſdaine :
Leaſt ſorrow lend me words and words expreſſe,
The manner of my pittie wanting paine.
If I might teach thee witte better it weare,
Though not to loue,yet loue to tell me ſo,
As teſtie ſick-men when their deaths be neere,
No newes but health from their Phiſitions know.
For if I ſhould diſpaire I ſhould grow madde,
And in my madneſſe might ſpeake ill of thee,
Now this ill wreſting world is growne ſo bad,
Madde ſlanderers by madde eares beleeued be.
   That I may not be ſo, nor thou be lyde,   (wide.
   Beare thine eyes ſtraight , though thy proud heart goe

141

IN faith I doe not loue thee with mine eyes,
  For they in thee a thouſand errors note,
But 'tis my heart that loues what they diſpiſe,
Who in diſpight of view is pleaſd to dote.
Nor are mine eares with thy toungs tune delighted,
Nor tender feeling to baſe touches prone,
Nor taſte, nor ſmell, deſire to be inuited
To any ſenſuall feaſt with thee alone :
But my fiue wits,nor my fiue ſences can
Diſwade one fooliſh heart from ſeruing thee,
Who leaues vnſwai'd the likeneſſe of a man,
Thy proud hearts ſlaue and vaſſall wretch to be :
   Onely my plague thus farre I count my gaine,
   That ſhe that makes me ſinne,awards me paine.

142

LOue is my sinne, and thy deare vertue hate,
Hate of my sinne, grounded on sinfull louing,
O but with mine, compare thou thine owne state,
And thou shalt finde it merrits not reproouing,
Or if it do, not from those lips of thine,
That haue prophan'd their scarlet ornaments,
And seald false bonds of loue as oft as mine,
Robd others beds reuenues of their rents.
Be it lawfull I loue thee as thou lou'st those,
Whome thine eyes wooe as mine importune thee,
Roote pittie in thy heart that when it growes,
Thy pitty may deserue to pittied bee.
   If thou doost seeke to haue what thou doost hide,
   By selfe example mai'st thou be denide.

143

LOe as a carefull huswife runnes to catch,
One of her fethered creatures broake away,
Sets downe her babe and makes all swift dispatch
In pursuit of the thing she would haue stay:
Whilst her neglected child holds her in chace,
Cries to catch her whose busie care is bent,
To follow that which flies before her face:
Not prizing her poore infants discontent;
So runst thou after that which flies from thee,
Whilst I thy babe chace thee a farre behind,
But if thou catch thy hope turne back to me:
And play the mothers part kisse me, be kind.
   So will I pray that thou maist haue thy *Will*,
   If thou turne back and my loude crying still.

144

TWo loues I haue of comfort and dispaire,
Which like two spirits do sugiest me still,
The better angell is a man right faire:
The worser spirit a woman collour'd il.
To win me soone to hell my femall euill,

Tempteth

Tempteth my better angel from my sight,
And would corrupt my saint to be a diuel:
Wooing his purity with her fowle pride.
And whether that my angel be turn'd finde,
Suspect I may, yet not directly tell,
But being both from me both to each friend,
I gesse one angel in an others hel.

 Yet this shal i nere know but liue in doubt,
 Till my bad angel fire my good one out.

145

THose lips that Loues owne hand did make,
Breath'd forth the sound that said I hate,
To me that languisht for her sake:
But when she saw my wofull state,
Straight in her heart did mercie come,
Chiding that tongue that euer sweet,
Was vsde in giuing gentle dome:
And tought it thus a new to greete:
I hate she alterd with an end,
That follow'd it as gentle day,
Doth follow night who like a fiend
From heauen to hell is flowne away.

 I hate, from hate away she threw,
 And sau'd my life saying not you.

146

POore soule the center of my sinfull earth,
My sinfull earth these rebbell powres that thee array,
Why dost thou pine within and suffer dearth
Painting thy outward walls so costlie gay?
Why so large cost hauing so short a lease,
Dost thou vpon thy fading mansion spend?
Shall wormes inheritors of this excesse,
Eate vp thy charge? is this thy bodies end?
Then soule liue thou vpon thy seruants losse,
And let that pine to aggrauat thy store;
Buy tearmes diuine in selling houres of drosse:

Within be fed, without be rich no more,
  So shalt thou feed on death, that feeds on men,
   And death once dead, ther's no more dying then.

147

MY loue is as a feauer longing still,
  For that which longer nurseth the disease,
Feeding on that which doth preserue the ill,
Th'vncertaine sicklie appetite to please:
My reason the Phisition to my loue,
Angry that his prescriptions are not kept
Hath left me, and I desperate now approoue,
Desire is death, which Phisick did except.
Past cure I am, now Reason is past care,
And frantick madde with euer-more vnrest,
My thoughts and my discourse as mad mens are,
At randon from the truth vainely exprest.
  For I haue sworne thee faire, and thought thee bright,
  Who art as black as hell, as darke as night.

148

O Me! what eyes hath loue put in my head,
  Which haue no correspondence with true sight,
Or if they haue, where is my iudgment fled,
That censures falsely what they see aright?
If that be faire whereon my false eyes dote,
What meanes the world to say it is not so?
If it be not, then loue doth well denote,
Loues eye is not so true as all mens, no,
How can it? O how can loues eye be true,
That is so vext with watching and with teares?
No maruaile then though I mistake my view,
The sunne it selfe sees not, till heauen cleeres.
  O cunning loue, with teares thou keepst me blinde,
  Least eyes well seeing thy foule faults should finde.

149

CAnst thou O cruell, say I loue thee not,
  When I against my selfe with thee pertake:

Doe

Doe I not thinke on thee when I forgot
Am of my selfe, all tirant for thy sake?
Who hateth thee that I doe call my friend,
On whom froun'st thou that I doe saune vpon,
Nay if thou lowrst on me doe I not spend
Reuenge vpon my selfe with present mone?
What merrit do I in my selfe respect,
That is so proude thy seruice to dispise,
When all my best doth worship thy defect,
Commanded by the motion of thine eyes.
   But loue hate on for now I know thy minde,
   Those that can see thou lou'st, and I am blind.

150

OH from what powre haft thou this powrefull might,
VVith insufficiency my heart to sway,
To make me giue the lie to my true sight,
And swere that brightnesse doth not grace the day?
Whence haft thou this becomming of things il,
That in the very refuse of thy deeds,
There is such strength and warrantie of skill,
That in my minde thy worst all best exceeds?
Who taught thee how to make me loue thee more,
The more I heare and see iust cause of hate,
Oh though I loue what others doe abhor,
VVith others thou shouldst not abhor my state.
   If thy vnworthinesse raisd loue in me,
   More worthy I to be belou'd of thee.

151

LOue is too young to know what conscience is,
Yet who knowes not conscience is borne of loue,
Then gentle cheater vrge not my amisse,
Leaft guilty of my faults thy sweet selfe proue.
For thou betraying me, I doe betray
My nobler part to my grose bodies treason,
My soule doth tell my body that he may,
Triumph in loue, flesh staies no farther reason,

Bus

But ryfing at thy name doth point out thee,
As his triumphant prize,proud of this pride,
He is contented thy poore drudge to be
To ftand in thy affaires,fall by thy fide.
   No want of confcience hold it that I call,
   Her loue, for whofe deare loue I rife and fall.

152

IN louing thee thou know'ft I am forfworne,
But thou art twice forfworne to me loue fwearing,
In act thy bed-vow broake and new faith torne,
In vowing new hate after new loue bearing:
But why of two othes breach doe I accufe thee,
When I breake twenty:I am periur'd moft,
For all my vowes are othes but to mifufe thee:
And all my honeft faith in thee is loft.
For I haue fworne deepe othes of thy deepe kindneffe:
Othes of thy loue,thy truth,thy conftancie,
And to inlighten thee gaue eyes to bliadneffe,
Or made them fwere againft the thing they fee.
   For I haue fworne thee faire:more periurde eye,
   To fwere againft the truth fo foule a lie.

153

CVpid laid by his brand and fell a fleepe,
A maide of *Dyans* this aduantage found,
And his loue-kindling fire did quickly fteepe
In a could vallie-fountaine of that ground:
Which borrowd from this holie fire of loue,
A dateleffe liuely heat ftill to indure,
And grew a feething bath which yet men proue,
Againft ftrang malladies a foueraigne cure:
But at my miftres eie loues brand new fired,
The boy for triall needes would touch my breft,
I fick withall the helpe of bath defired,
And thether hied a fad diftemperd gueft.
   But found no cure,the bath for my helpe lies,
   Where *Cupid* got new fire;my miftres eye.

THe little Loue-God lying once a fleepe,
  Laid by his fide his heart inflaming brand,
Whilft many Nymphes that vou'd chaft life to keep,
Came tripping by,but in her maiden hand,
The fayreft votary tooke vp that fire,
Which many Legions of true hearts had warm'd,
And fo the Generall of hot defire,
Was fleeping by a Virgin hand difarm'd.
This brand fhe quenched in a coole Well by,
Which from loues fire tooke heat perpetuall,
Growing a bath and healthfull remedy,
For men difeafd,but I my Miftriffe thrall,
    Came there for cure and this by that I proue,
    Loues fire heates water,water cooles not loue.

FINIS.

K   A

A Louers complaint.

BY

WILLIAM SHAKE-SPEARE.

FRom off a hill whose concaue wombe reworded,
A plaintfull story from a sistring vale
My spirrits t'attend this doble voyce accorded,
And downe I laid to list the sad tun'd tale,
Ere long espied a sickle maid full pale
Tearing of papers breaking rings a twaine,
Storming her world with sorrowes, wind and raine.

Vpon her head a plattid hiue of straw,
Which fortified her visage from the Sunne,
Whereon the thought might thinke sometime it saw
The carkas of a beauty spent and donne,
Time had not sithed all that youth begun,
Nor youth all quit, but spight of heauens fell rage,
Some beauty peept, through lettice of sear'd age.

Oft did she heaue her Napkin to her eyne,
Which on it had conceited charecters:
Laundring the silken figures in the brine,
That seasoned woe had pelleted in teares,
And often reading what contents it beares:
As often shriking vndistinguisht wo,
In clamours of all size both high and low.

Some-times her leueld eyes their carriage ride,
As they did battry to the spheres intend:
Sometime diuerted their poore balls are tide,
To th'orbed earth; sometimes they do extend,
Their view right on, anon their gases lend,

To euery place at once and no where fixt,
The mind and ſight diſtractedly commxit.

Her haire nor looſe nor ti'd in formall plat,
Proclaimd in her a careleſſe hand of pride;
For ſome vntuck'd deſcended her ſheu'd hat,
Hanging her pale and pined cheeke beſide,
Some in her threeden fillet ſtill did bide,
And trew to bondage would not breake from thence,
Though ſlackly braided in looſe negligence.

A thouſand fauours from a maund ſhe drew,
Of amber chriſtall and of bedded Iet,
Which one by one ſhe in a riuer threw,
Vpon whoſe weeping margent ſhe was ſet,
Like vſery applying wet to wet,
Or Monarches hands that lets not bounty fall,
Where want cries ſome;but where exceſſe begs all.

Of folded ſchedulls had ſhe many a one,
Which ſhe peruſ d,ſighd,tore and gaue the fiud,
Crackt many a ring of Poſied gold and bone,
Bidding them find their Sepulchers in mud,
Found yet mo letters ſadly pend in blood,
With ſleided ſilke,ſeate and affectedly
Enſwath'd and ſeald to curious ſecrecy.

Theſe often bath'd ſhe in her fluxiue eies,
And often kiſt,and often gaue to teare,
Cried O falſe blood thou regiſter of lies,
What vnapproued witnes dooſt thou beare!
Inke would haue ſeem'd more blacke and damned heare
This ſaid in top of rage the lines ſhe rents,
Big diſcontent,ſo breaking their contents.

A reuerend man that graz'd his cattell ny,
        R 2.   Some

Sometime a bluſ-erer that the ruffle knew
Of Court of Cittie, and had let go by
The ſwifteſt houres obſerued as they flew,
Towards this afflicted fancy faſtly drew:
And priuiledg'd by age deſires to know
In breefe the grounds and motiues of her wo.

So ſlides he downe vppon his greyned bat;
And comely diſtant ſits he by her ſide,
When hee againe deſires her, being ſatte,
Her greeuance with his hearing to deuide:
If that from him there may be ought applied
Which may her ſuffering extaſie aſſwage
Tis promiſt in the charitie of age.

Father ſhe ſaies, though in mee you behold
The iniury of many a blaſting houre;
Let it not tell your Iudgement I am old,
Not age, but ſorrow, ouer me hath power;
I might as yet haue bene a ſpreading flower
Freſh to my ſelfe, if I had ſelfe applyed
Loue to my ſelfe, and to no Loue beſide.

But wo is mee, too early I atttended
A youthfull ſuit it was to gaine my grace;
O one by natures outwards ſo commended,
That maidens eyes ſtucke ouer all his face,
Loue lackt a dwelling and made him her place,
And when in his faire parts ſhee didde abide,
Shee was new lodg'd and newly Deified.

His browny locks did hang in crooked curles,
And euery light occaſion of the wind
Vpon his lippes their ſilken parcels hurles,
Whats ſweet to do, to do wil aptly find,
Each eye that ſaw him did inchaunt the minde:

For

For on his viſage was in little drawne,
What largeneſſe thinkes in parradiſe was ſawne.

Smal ſhew of man was yet vpon his chinne,
His phenix downe began but to appeare
Like vnſhorne veluet, on that termleſſe skin
Whoſe bare out-brag'd the web it ſeem'd to were.
Yet ſhewed his viſage by that coſt more deare,
And nice affections wauering ſtood in doubt
If beſt were as it was, or beſt without.

His qualities were beautious as his forme,
For maiden tongu'd he was and thereof free;
Yet if men mou'd him, was he ſuch a ſtorme
As oft twixt May and Aprill is to ſee,
When windes breath ſweet, vnruly though they bee.
His rudeneſſe ſo with his authoriz'd youth,
Did liuery falſeneſſe in a pride of truth.

Wel could hee ride, and often men would ſay
That horſe his mettell from his rider takes
Proud of ſubiection, noble by the ſwaie,   (makes
What rounds, what bounds, what courſe what ſtop he
And controuerſie hence a queſtion takes,
Whether the horſe by him became his deed,
Or he his mannad'g, by'th wel doing Steed.

But quickly on this ſide the verdict went,
His reall habitude gaue life and grace
To appertainings and to ornament,
Accompliſht in him-ſelfe not in his caſe:
All ayds them-ſelues made fairer by their place,
Can for addicions, yet their purpoſ'd trimme
Peec'd not his grace but were al grac'd by him.

So on the tip of his ſubduing tongue.

All kinde of arguments and question deepe,
Al replication prompt, and reason ftrong
For his aduantage ftill did wake and fleep,
To make the weeper laugh, the laugher weepe
He hadthe dialect and different skil,
Catching al paffions in his craft of will.

That hee didde in the general bofome raigne
Of young, of old, and fexes both inchanted,
To dwel with him in thoughts, or to remaine
In perfonal duty, following where he haunted,
Confent's bewitcht, ere he defire haue granted,
And dialogu'd for him what he would fay,
Askt their own wils and made their wils obey.

Many there were that did his picture gette
To ferue their eies, and in it put their mind,
Like fooles that in th' imagination fet
The goodly obiects which abroad they find
Oflands and manfions, theirs in thought affign'd,
And labouring in moe pleafures to beftow them,
Then the true gouty Land-lord which doth owe them.

So many haue that neuer toucht his hand
Sweetly fuppos'd them miftreffe of his heart:
My wofull felfe that did in freedome ftand,
And was my owne fee fimple (not in part)
What with his art in youth and youth in art
Threw my affections in his charmed power,
Referu'd the ftalke and gaue him al my flower.

Yet did I not as fome my equals did
Demaund of him, nor being defired yeelded,
Finding my felfe in honour fo forbidde,
With fafeft diftance I mine honour fheelded,
Experience for me many bulwarkes builded

Of proofs new bleeding which remaind the foile
Of this false Iewell, and his amorous spoile.

But ah who euer shun'd by precedent,
The destin'd ill she must her selfe assay,
Or forc'd examples gainst her owne content
To put the by-past perrils in her way?
Counsaile may stop a while what will not stay:
For when we rage, aduise is often seene
By blunting vs to make our wits more keene.

Nor giues it satisfaction to our blood,
That wee must curbe it vppon others proofe,
To be forbod the sweets that seemes so good,
For seare of harmes that preach in our behoofe;
O appetite from iudgement stand aloofe!
The one a pallate hath that needs will taste,
Though reason weepe and cry it is thy last.

For further I could say this mans vntrue,
And knew the patternes of his soule beguiling,
Heard where his plants in others Orchards grew,
Saw how deceits were guilded in his smiling,
Knew vowes, were euer brokers to defiling,
Thought Characters and words meerly but art,
And bastards of his soule adulterat heart.

And long vpon these termes I held my Citty,
Till thus hee gan besiege me : Gentle maid
Haue of my suffering youth some feeling pitty
And be not of my holy vowes affraid,
Thats to ye sworne to none was euer said,
For feasts of loue I haue bene call'd vnto
Till now did nere inuite nor neuer vovv.

All my offences that abroad you see
                    K 4   Are

Are errors of the blood none of the mind:
Loue made them not,with acture they may be,
Where neither Party is nor trew nor kind,
They fought their fhame that fo their fhame did find,
And fo much leffe of fhame in me remaines,
By how much of me their reproch containes,

Among the many that mine eyes haue feene,
Not one whofe flame my hart fo much as warmed,
Or my affection put to th, fmalleft teene,
Or any of my leifures euer Charmed,
Harme haue I done to them but nere was harmed,
Kept hearts in liueries,but mine owne was free,
And raignd commaunding in his monarchy.

Looke heare what tributes wounded fancies fent me,
Of palyd pearles and rubies red as blood:
Figuring that they their paffions likewife lent me
Of greefe and blufhes, aptly vnderftood
In bloodleffe white,and the encrimfon'd mood,
Effects of terror and deare modefty,
Encampt in hearts but fighting outwardly.

And Lo behold thefe tallents of their heir,
With twifted mettle amoroufly empleacht
I haue receau'd from many a feueral faire,
Their kind acceptance, wepingly befeecht,
With th'annexions of faire gems inricht,
And deepe brain'd fonnets that did amplifie
Each ftones deare Nature,worth and quallity.

The Diamond?why twas beautifull and hard,
Whereto his inuif'd properties did tend,
The deepe greene Emrald in whofe frefh regard,
Weake fights their fickly radience do amend.
The heauen hewd Saphir and the Opall blend

With

With obiects manyfold ; each seuerall stone,
With wit well blazond smil'd or made some mone.

Lo all these trophies of affections hot,
Of pensiu'd and subdew'd desires the tender,
Nature hath chargd me that I hoord them not,
But yeeld them vp where I my selfe must render:
That is to you my origin and ender :
For these of force must your oblations be,
Since I their Aulter, you en patrone me.

Oh then aduance(of yours)that phraseles hand,
Whose white weighes downe the airy scale of praise,
Take all these similies to your owne command,
Hollowed with sighes that burning lunges did raise:
What me your minister for you obaies
Workes vnder you,and to your audit comes
Their distract parcells,in combined summes.

Lo this deuice was sent me from a Nun,
Or Sister sanctified of holiest note,
Which late her noble suit in court did shun,
Whose rarest hauings made the blossoms dote,
For she was sought by spirits of ritchest cote,
But kept cold distance,and did thence remoue,
To spend her liuing in eternall loue.

But oh my sweet what labour ist to leaue,
The thing we haue not,mastring what not striues,
Playing the Place which did no forme receiue,
Playing patient sports in vnconstraind giues,
She that her fame so to her selfe contriues,
The scarres of battaile scapeth by the flight,
And makes her absence valiant,not her might.

Oh pardon me in that my boast is true,

L   The

The accident which brought me to her eie,
Vpon the moment did her force subdewe,
And now she would the caged cloister flie:
Religious loue put out religions eye:
Not to be tempted would she be enur'd,
And now to tempt all liberty procure.

How mightie then you are, Oh heare me tell,
The broken bosoms that to me belong,
Haue emptied all their fountaines in my well:
And mine I powre your Ocean all amonge:
I strong ore them and you ore me being strong,
Must for your victorie vs all congest,
As compound loue to phisick your cold brest.

My parts had powre to charme a sacred Sunne,
Who disciplin'd I dieted in grace,
Beleeu'd her eies, when they t' assaile begun,
All vowes and consecrations giuing place:
O most potentiall loue, vowe, bond, nor space
In thee hath neither sting, knot, nor confine
For thou art all and all things els are thine.

When thou impressest what are precepts worth
Of stale example? when thou wilt inflame,
How coldly those impediments stand forth
Of wealth of filliall feare, lawe, kindred fame,   (shame
Loues armes are peace, gainst rule, gainst sence, gainst
And sweetens in the suffring pangues it beares,
The *Alloes* of all forces, shockes and feares.

Now all these hearts that doe on mine depend,
Feeling it breake, with bleeding groanes they pine,
And supplicant their sighes to you extend
To leaue the battrie that you make gainst mine,
Lending soft audience, to my sweet designe,

                                                    And

And credent soule,to that strong bonded oth,
That shall preferre and vndertake my troth.

This said,his watrie eies he did dismount,
Whose sightes till then were leaueld on my face,
Each cheeke a riuer running from a fount,
With brynish currant downe-ward flowed a pace:
Oh how the channell to the streame gaue gracel
Who glaz'd with Christall gate the glowing Roses,
That flame through water which their hew incloses,

Oh father,what a hell of witch-craft lies,
In the small orb of one perticular teare?
But with the invndation of the eies:
What rocky heart to water will not weare?
What brest so cold that is not warmed heare,
Or cleft effect,cold modesty hot wrath:
Both fire from hence,and chill extincture hath.

For loe his passion but an art of craft,
Euen there resolu'd my reason into teares,
There my white stole of chastity I daft,
Shooke off my sober gardes,and ciuill feares,
Appeare to him as he to me appeares:
All melting,though our drops this diffrence bore,
His poifon'd me, and mine did him restore.

In him a plenitude of subtle matter,
Applied to Cautills,all straing formes receiues,
Of burning blushes,or of weeping water,
Or sounding palenesse: and he takes and leaues,
In eithers aptnesse as it best deceiues:
To blush at speeches ranck,to weepe at woes
Or to turne white and sound at tragick showes.

That not a heart which in his leuell came,

L 3   Could

Cou'd scape the haile of his all hurting ayme,
Shewing faire Nature is both kinde and tame :
And vaild in them did winne whom he would maime,
Against the thing he sought,he would exclaime,
When he most burnt in hart-wisht luxurie,
He preacht pure maide,and praisd cold chastitie.

Thus meerely with the garment of a grace,
The naked and concealed feind he couerd,
That th'vnexperient gaue the tempter place,
Which like a Cherubin aboue them houerd,
Who young and simple would not be so louerd.
Aye me I fell, and yet do question make,
What I should doe againe for such a sake.

O that infected moysture of his eye,
O that false fire which in his cheeke so glowd:
O that forc'd thunder from his heart did flye,
O that sad breath his spungie lungs bestowed,
O all that borrowed motion seeming owed,
Would yet againe betray the fore-betrayed,
And new peruert a reconciled Maide.

FINIS.